ALSO BY MISS READ

Village School
Village Diary
Storm in the Village
Thrush Green
Winter in Thrush Green
Over the Gate
Miss Clare Remembers
The Market Square
The Howards of Caxley
The Fairacre Festival
News from Thrush Green
Emily Davis
Tyler's Row
Miss Read's Christmas
(*Village Christmas* and *The Christmas Mouse*)
Farther Afield

Miss Read's

Country Cooking
OR
TO CUT A CABBAGE-LEAF

ACADEMY CHICAGO PUBLISHERS
1992

Published in 1992 by
Academy Chicago Publishers
213 West Institute Place
Chicago, Illinois 60610

Copyright © Miss Read, 1969
New illustrations copyright © Sally Seymour, 1985

First published by Michael Joseph Ltd, 1969.

Printed and bound in the U.S.A. by The Haddon Craftsmen, Inc.

Library of Congress Cataloging-in-Publication Data

Read, Miss
    Miss Read's country cooking, or, To cut a cabbage-leaf
       p.   cm
    Originally published: London : Joseph, 1969.
    Includes index
    ISBN 0-89733-373-X
    1. Cookery, English. I. Title. II. Country cooking.
    III. Title: To cut a cabbage-leaf.
TX717.R37 1992
    641.5—dc20   92-6865
                                                  CIP

To Sheila
With love from her godmother

Contents

Autumn

Winter

ACKNOWLEDGEMENTS

My thanks are due to the following for permission to reproduce extracts from works in which they hold the copyright:

David Higham Associates Ltd., *Country Fare* by Mary Aylett, and *French Provincial Cooking* by Elizabeth David; Kent Archaeological Society, article in *Archaeologica Cantiana XLVI* Methuen & Co. Ltd. and The Bodleian Library, Oxford, *The Wind in the Willows* by Kenneth Grahame; National Trade Press Ltd., *Diary of a Farmer's Wife* by Anne Hughes; Thomas Nelson & Sons Ltd., *Cunning Cookery* by Geoffrey Boumphrey; Oxford University Press, World's Classics, *Diary of a Country Parson* by James Woodforde; Ward Lock & Co. Ltd., *Mrs Beeton's Cookery and Household Management* (1960 edition).

So she went into the garden to cut a cabbage-leaf, to make an apple pie; and at the same time a great she-bear, coming up the street, pops its head into the shop. 'What! no soap?' So he died, and she very imprudently married the barber; and there were present the Picninnies, and the Joblillies, and the Garyalies, and the grand Panjandrum himself, with the little round button at top, and they all fell to playing the game of catch as catch can, till the gunpowder ran out at the heels of the boots.

SAMUEL FOOTE 1720–1777

Weights and Measures

The recipes in this book give English weights and measures. Americans like to use cupfuls in their recipes, and the ½ pint measuring cup used in America is the equivalent of 2/5 of an Imperial pint, because:

The British Imperial pint = 20 fluid oz
The American pint = 16 fluid oz

Substance	British Measuring Cup	American Measuring Cup
Flour	1 cup = 5 oz	1 cup = 4 oz
Caster sugar	1 cup = 9 oz	1 cup = 8 oz

Similarly, the American tablespoon and teaspoon are slightly smaller than the British ones. A British Standard tablespoon measures 1 fluid ounce.

The following tables show comparative amounts. They show *level* Standard Measuring spoons.

Substance	British Spoon	American Spoon
Flour	3 tabs. = 1 oz	4 tabs. = 1 oz
Caster sugar	2 tabs. = 1¼ oz	2 tabs. = 1 oz
Butter	2 tabs. = 1¼ oz	2 tabs. = 1 oz
Powdered gelatine	4 tsp. = ½ oz	5 tsp. = ½ oz

This list of Solid Measure should be useful in converting British measures into American ones.

British	American
1 lb flour	4 cups
1 lb caster sugar	2 cups
1 lb butter or lard	2 cups
1 lb brown sugar	2½ cups
1 lb rice	2 cups
1 lb minced meat	2 cups
1 lb soft breadcrumbs	4 cups
1 oz golden syrup	1 level measuring tablespoon
1 oz sugar	,, ,, ,,
½ oz butter	,, ,, ,,

Before long we shall be using the *metric system* for our weights and measures and it is as well to get used to the basic changes.

Approximate equivalents are:

$$1 \text{ oz} = 30 \text{ grammes}$$
$$\tfrac{1}{4} \text{ lb} = 114 \text{ grammes}$$
$$\tfrac{1}{2} \text{ lb} = 228 \text{ grammes}$$
$$1 \text{ lb} = 454 \text{ grammes}$$
$$1 \text{ } kilogramme = 2 \text{ lbs } 2\tfrac{1}{2} \text{ oz}$$

Liquid Measures

$$1 \text{ gill} = 0\cdot142 \text{ litre}$$
$$\tfrac{1}{2} \text{ Imperial pint (10 fluid oz)} = 0\cdot284 \text{ litre}$$
$$1 \text{ Imperial pint} = 0\cdot568 \text{ litre}$$
$$1\tfrac{3}{4} \text{ Imperial pint} = 1 \text{ litre}$$

Note: Amounts given in these recipes are for 4–6 people.

Introduction

'Do you think', asked my publisher, when I first suggested this book, 'that you are *greedy* enough to write a cookery book?'

It would have been more delicate, I felt, to use the phrase 'interested in food' rather than 'greedy'. It sounds so much more rarefied, and I am vain enough to hope that it would be nearer the truth.

For, I'm happy to admit, that food fascinates me. 'We are what we eat', say some, which is a pretty sobering thought. Do cannibals really imbibe, as they hope, the courage of their victims as they tackle a brave late-enemy's heart? Are vegetarians less bloodthirsty than carnivores? Does a heavy consumption of milk make one bovine in outlook? And what's all this one hears about honey being an aphrodisiac?

There is still a modicum of black magic mixed up with our ideas of nutrition, and I, for one, enjoy the relics of ancient folk lore which still crop up in cookery books.

Certainly, there are many snippets of country wisdom which present-day cooks would do well to heed. Celery and brussel sprouts, for instance, *are* better after frost. Blackberries *are* always nicer in September than October, for in the latter month, as every country child knows, the Devil trails his coat over the fruit and spoils it!

It is this interest in food, which so many of us enjoy, which makes memorable dozens of literary meals. Do you remember Mr Woodhouse in 'Emma'? One might almost think of him as the arch-priest of *non-eating*.

'A small basin of thin gruel' writes Jane Austen, 'was all that he could, with thorough self-approbation, recommend.' He did however propose to Mrs Bates at one supper party that she venture on an egg – a very small one. 'One of our small eggs will not hurt you.' Luckily, Emma was dispensing minced chicken and scalloped oysters throughout her father's anxious pleadings, so that the guests were adequately refreshed.

As for Parson Woodforde, who was rector of Weston Longe-
ville from 1774 until his death in 1803, his diary fairly bursts with
food. Listen to this June dinner at his wealthy neighbour's
house.

'Dinner boiled Tench, Peas Soup, a Couple of Boiled Chicken
and Pigs Face, hashed Calf's Head, Beans, and rosted Rump of
Beef with New Potatoes etc. 2nd Course rosted Duck and green
Peas, a very fine Leveret rosted, Strawberry Cream, Jelly,
Puddings etc. Desert – Strawberries, Cherries and last Years
nonpareils.'

Or this, for fifteen people.

'We had for dinner a boiled Rump Beef 45 pd. weight, a Ham
and half a dozen fowls, a roasted Saddle of Mutton, two very
rich puddings, and a good Sallet with a fine cucumber . . . '

No wonder that the good parson often has recourse to 'a dose
of Rhubarb before retiring.' And one of the most poignant en-
tries in the diary, commenting on a sleepless night of indigestion,
consists of these four succinct words: 'Mince Pye rose oft.'

But the interesting thing to note, after one has got over the
sheer stupefying bulk of the meals, is the large proportion of
meat eaten. How different is the picture drawn by Flora Thompson a hundred years or so later! It is true that the labourer's
home was a modest one compared with the parson's, but the
main meal simply consisted of a tiny cube of bacon from their
own pig, any vegetables available from the garden, including
potatoes, and a roly-poly pudding tied in a cloth and made
from flour from the gleanings at harvest-time.

All went into the pot together and were dished up when the
man of the house came home from the fields and the children
back from school. The bacon amounted 'to little more than a
taste each.' They filled up empty corners at other times with
bread and lard, or bread and home-made jam. Milk and eggs,
which one might have thought plentiful, were extremely scarce.
When one considers the length of a man's working day, and the
tough conditions he endured – ploughing a vast field of North
Oxfordshire clay on foot behind a team of horses would have
made even Mr Woodhouse hungry – it is amazing how little
food they managed upon.

I suppose that the moral to be drawn from this is that 'the rough plenty of the poor', if plenty you can call it, was wholesome food. The pig was well-fed, sometimes better fed than the children. The vegetables and fruit were nourished by natural organic matter, and the nearest the cabbages got to spraying was a bowlful of washing-up water cast over them from the back door, interspersed with rain showers. When the housewife-cook wanted to prepare the meal 'she went down the garden to cut a cabbage leaf' and it was in the bubbling water within minutes, fresh, firm and fragrant. The tired produce which we are so often forced to buy would have been chucked into the pig's sty to make future bacon. Lettuces, pearly spring onions, crisp radishes, all would be plucked from the soil, washed and eaten within the hour. And always, no matter how poor the garden, there would be a few herbs to add relish and piquancy to the monotony of the diet.

After a sad period of neglect it is good to see a revival of interest in herbs and spices. I have put in a list of those most useful to the cook, and hope that readers will experiment.

This cookery book has many short-comings. It does not supply, as so many more ambitious books do, those lovely recipes for furniture polish and cough-cure at the end. Nor does it tell you how to engage a parlour-maid or how to order your dry-goods quarterly.

And just because it is called 'Country Cooking' please don't expect this book to be aggressively bucolic. You won't find any of the 'take-a-calf's-head-cleanse-nostrils-remove-tongue' type of recipe here, for the simple reason that I cannot face such horrors. Nor will you find any of those dainty recipes about crystallizing rose petals – a two-day procedure as far as I can see – for I think that most of us prefer to buy half an ounce when needed – perhaps every tenth year or so – and reckon the money prudently spent.

Similarly, it is not all syllabub-and-cottage-pie (though you will find recipes for these two delectable dishes). We live in times when the produce of the whole world is available to us, at a price, and our tastes are sophisticated. There are recipes here from all manner of countries and climes, and in the deep freezers about us are their excellent ingredients which Providence has supplied and we are glad to use. As Michael Flanders' cannibal chief says: 'If the Ju-ju hadn't meant us to eat people he wouldn't have made us of meat.'

Let us use the produce available, by all means, but don't let us lose sight, amidst the welter of exotic out-of-season food which tempts us, the satisfaction of cooking meat, fruit and vegetables in season when they are at their freshest, cheapest, and most delectable and when our bodies are most keenly refreshed by, and responsive to them, as our forebears knew well. That is why these recipes are arranged under 'Seasons'.

We are all inheritors of what has gone before, and this truth is most sharply felt by anyone writing a cookery book. To all the cooks before me, and to my many friends whose handiwork I have enjoyed and whose recipes appear here, I gratefully acknowledge my debt.

Spring

After the semi-hibernation of winter, the cold and the darkness, the chilblains and the coughs, we long for fresh air and sunshine. Do you remember Mole in *The Wind in the Willows* who felt the urge so strongly that he flung down his whitewash brush and fought his way upward, 'muttering to himself, "Up we go! Up we go!" till at last, pop! his snout came out into the sunlight, and he found himself rolling in the warm grass of a great meadow'.

Soon afterwards, you remember, he encountered the Water Rat, who took him sculling on the sparkling river. At lunch time he produced a wicker hamper.

' "What's inside it?" asked the Mole.

"There's cold chicken inside it," replied the Rat briefly; "coldtonguecoldhamcoldbeefpickledgherkinssaladfrenchrolls cresssandwidgespottedmeatgingerbeerlemonadesodawater . . ."

"O stop stop," cried Mole in ecstasies. "This is too much!" '

And though Rat assured him that his friends often told him he was 'a mean beast and cut it *very* fine!' we would probably agree with Mole.

We can sympathize with his excitement, too. Let's get out! Let's try something new! Our senses are ready for stimulants. We want sunlight, primroses, birds singing, something new to wear and, above all, something new to eat.

Luckily, from the cook's point of view, there is plenty to offer palates jaded with root vegetables, frozen peas and broccoli spears, stews, pies, thick soups and all the everyday winter dishes. Fresh salmon is in season, mackerel, shrimps and whitebait are at their best, and although our own fruit has not yet appeared, young vegetables are beginning to come on in the garden, and the mint and parsley is beginning to spring anew.

Citrus fruits are plentiful and eggs, too. Now is the time to make lemon curd and to try out all those egg dishes which never seemed quite substantial enough in frosty weather. And don't forget that ducklings and spring chickens are now appearing to add to all the other hopeful ingredients of Spring.

Herbs

Our ancestors knew far more about the use of herbs, both for flavouring their dishes and curing their bodily disorders, than ever we can hope to know. Luckily, there is a revival of interest in the lore of herbs, and many a town-dweller, forced to live many floors above ground, has a flowerpot or two with mint and parsley growing on the window-sill. Those with gardens know how rewarding it is to snip their own chives, or pick their own leaves from the bay tree, flourishing in the fresh air.

Here are a few which are easy to grow, and a fine adjunct to all manner of dishes.

Basil

A mild herb which combines well with tomatoes, fish, liver, duck and venison. It is at its finest in August, when it can be dried and stored for winter use.

Bay Leaves

These may be used for their rather nutty flavour, and go well with sauces and gravies, and casserole dishes, particularly of beef. A bay leaf is one of the necessary ingredients of a bouquet garni.

Bouquet Garni

This consists of a small bunch of herbs tied together either with string, or in a muslin bag, which can be easily removed when the cooking is complete. The usual ingredients are a sprig of thyme, two sprigs of parsley and a bay leaf. Other additions such as basil, marjoram or a crushed clove of garlic, can be added if the dish is improved by so doing.

Chives

One of the most useful herbs to grow, and best used freshly cut. It combines well with most foods, but its mild onion-like flavour is particularly good with cream cheese and as a garnish to salads, sauces and some white soups. They also blend well in an omelette or with scrambled eggs.

Fennel

Its fine foliage is attractive in the herb garden. Its flavour is that of aniseed. The feathery leaves, snipped finely, add a piquant touch to salads, or can be blended with butter for savoury spreads. Its main use in the kitchen is for flavouring fish sauces.

Garlic

This is of the same family as the onion, chive and leek, but possesses a most powerful aroma and taste. Its strength is greater when the dish in which it is used is heated. Use sparingly. When a recipe calls for 'a crushed clove of garlic', remove one section of the bulb, chop finely, sprinkle with a little salt and crush flat with the blade of a knife. It is best to keep a special small garlic board or tile for this job, as garlic can impregnate a working surface fairly easily.

Garlic is used in soup, fish and meat dishes, and a salad bowl rubbed with the cut surface of a clove gives a pleasant tang to its ingredients.

Marjoram

There are four kinds of this herb, but the one used in the kitchen is called *Origanum Marjorana*. It has a wide variety of uses, but is rather strongly aromatic, so use with discretion. It blends well with pâté, sauces, stews, and stuffings, particularly for poultry, and combines with onion very agreeably.

Mint

We all know about mint in cooking. Its medicinal properties have been valued for centuries. Nicholas Culpeper, the famous herbalist who died in 1645, has this to say about *Mentha Viridis*:

'It is a herb of Venus. The juice taken in vinegar, stays bleeding, stirs up venery, or bodily lust; two or three branches taken in the juice of four pomegranates, stays the hiccough, vomiting, and allays the choler.' And much, much more!

Mrs Beeton herself points out that mint 'has the property of correcting flatulence, hence the custom of using it in pea-soup and with new potatoes'.

As well as these well-known uses, try it as one of the ingredients of stuffing for poultry for a change, and remember that a small sprig as a garnish to a citrus fruit dish, such as grape-fruit cocktail, can be very refreshing.

Myrrh or Chervil

This is more widely used in French cooking than in English. It tastes rather like parsley and is easy to grow. It can be used in much the same way as a flavouring agent for soups and sauces. It has a pretty leaf, and small sprigs can be used as a garnish to cold dishes and salads.

Parsley

This obliging herb goes with almost all dishes and provides an attractive garnish with its bright green feathery foliage.

If you want to dry it for winter use, gather it when young, blanch it for a minute in boiling water, and let it dry in a hot oven. When dry, rub it through a sieve and put the powder into an airtight jar.

They say, in these parts, that if parsley flourishes in the garden then it's a sure sign that the wife rules the house. It is also said of mint!

Rosemary

This is another very strongly aromatic herb and must be used with care. It goes well with mutton and lamb, poultry and game. Pea, spinach, chicken and turtle soups take rosemary well.

Always remove rosemary sprigs before serving a dish in which they have been used, and take care that none of the small spiky leaves remain embedded.

Sage

The Arabs say, so I am told, that if you want to live for ever you should eat sage every day. This is another strong herb – too strong for me, personally – and should be treated with respect. Ideal with onions, of course, and marrying happily with pork dishes, and in stuffings, particularly of duck and goose. Some people like tangy cheeses, of the cream variety, flavoured with sage.

Tarragon

'If you are buying tarragon plants for the garden, make sure you get the variety known as True French', advises Mrs Elizabeth David. This herb is one of the most useful ones, and the aromatic leaves when steeped for a short time in the appropriate liquor, impart their flavour to soups and sauces. It blends well with chicken, fish and egg dishes.

If you want to make your own tarragon vinegar, pick sprigs and place in a bottle of wine vinegar. They can stay in the vinegar indefinitely.

Thyme

There are many varieties of this tiny pungent plant. The one used in the kitchen is *Thymus vulgaris*, and goes well in stuffings, such as the well-known blend of thyme, parsley and lemon stuffing for poultry. It can be used to advantage in pork dishes, in liver pâté and is, of course, one of the ingredients of the bouquet garni. Use sparingly. It is another really strong herb.

Useful Spices

Allspice

This is not, as you might be forgiven for thinking, a mixture of spices, but a dried berry which is supposed to combine the flavour of cinnamon, nutmeg and cloves. It grows in the West Indies.

It can be used whole to flavour boiled meats or when marinading fish or in making pickles. In its powdered form it can be added to cakes, mincemeat and Christmas pudding.

Cinnamon

A much-neglected spice, in my opinion. Subtler than ginger, it can often replace it to advantage in cakes, for instance, particularly those using black treacle, and it is really far pleasanter sprinkled on fresh melon than the powdered ginger which so often burns the tongue.

It is the bark of a type of laurel tree which grows in the Far East. It comes in stick or powdered form, and is useful in flavouring hot drinks (milk stirred with a cinnamon stick is delicious), punches, creams, custards, cakes and pear and apple dishes. It is also used in pickles and chutneys.

My mother used to make a delicious cinnamon sponge cake, based on a Victoria sponge recipe. The recipe can be found in the Cakes section under Spring.

Cloves

One of the most aromatic spices, and needs to be used sparingly. I once encountered an apple pie in which there were so many cloves that I can only imagine that the inexperienced cook had flung in a fistful. Never a dedicated clove-fancier, that traumatic experience has put me off cloves for life, but used correctly they can provide a pleasant flavour to both sweet and savoury dishes.

They are the dried buds of a type of tropical myrtle, and the name derives from the Latin *clavus* meaning nail, referring to its shape.

They can be used for marinades of meat and game, stuck in an onion for meat stews, in pickles and curries, as well as in apple pies, puddings and cakes. In their ground form, for the last two, of course.

Ginger

One of the most useful and popular spices, it comes from the East Indies and Jamaica. In cooking it is usually used in its powdered form, although the addition of a little finely-chopped preserved ginger to gingerbread or ginger pudding makes both more delectable.

It is used in the pickling of fruit and preserves, adds a tang to such jams as rhubarb, and to marmalade.

You will find a reliable recipe for gingerbread and one for gingernuts in the Cakes section. Did you know that years ago ginger nuts were rolled into little balls the size of a walnut, and then baked? That is how the name came into being.

Mace

This can be bought in ground or blade form. It is the outer covering of the nutmeg, but is much milder in taste. It is useful for pâtés and stuffings and some meat dishes. It can be used, instead of nutmeg, to flavour mashed potato, and it is one of the ingredients of pickles and chutneys.

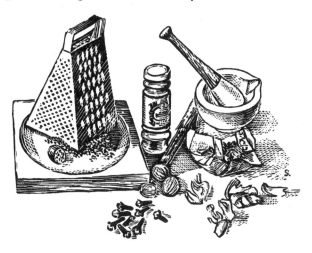

Nutmeg

'Hard aromatic spheroidal seed got from fruit of evergreen E-Indian tree,' says the Concise Oxford Dictionary. It deserves its popularity in the kitchen for it blends well with so many dishes, notably egg, those made of minced meat, creamed and mashed potatoes, as well as flavouring milk puddings, hot milk and spiced drinks, cakes, biscuits and puddings.

Pepper

There are many varieties of this most useful spice.

Black peppercorns, freshly ground, are milder in taste than white and are the best to use in the kitchen. *White* pepper is much hotter, and should be used sparingly. Remember that pepper, when ground, loses some of its flavour.

Cayenne pepper is very hot indeed.

Paprika is much less pungent than cayenne and comes from Hungary. It is useful not only in such dishes as pâtés, but because of its mild nature is useful for sprinkling on canapés, on cream cheese, white soups, etc., where its bright red colour shows to advantage.

Jamaica pepper is the name once used for the spice we now term *allspice*, mentioned first in this list.

Vanilla

This is the fruit of a tropical orchid and has been popular as a flavouring for centuries. It came originally from Mexico. Most kitchens have a little bottle of essence of vanilla and a drop or two of this concentrated form adds attraction to creams, chocolate dishes, soufflés, puddings and cakes.

The flavour is even better, I think, if a dried vanilla pod is kept permanently in a screw-top jar full of caster sugar, and this scented and flavoured sugar is used in the cooking of the above-mentioned dishes. Any good grocer has these long dark dried pods, nicely corked in long tubular glass containers. The sugar jar can be topped up again after use, and the vanilla pods will be a real investment for many months.

Game and Poultry in Season

Blackcock	August to December 10
Chickens	All the year round
Spring chickens	March to May
Ducklings	March to August
Ducks	August to March
Wild ducks	August to March 15
Geese	September to February. Best at Michaelmas
Goslings	February to September
Grouse	August 12 to December 10
Guinea Fowl	February to August
Hares	September to March 1
Leverets	September to February
Partridges	September 1 to February 1
Pheasants	October 1 to March 1
Pigeons	All the year
Snipe	August 1 to March 1
Teal	August 1 to March 1

TURKEYS	September to March. Best in December
VENISON	May to January
WOODCOCK	August 1 to March 1

More and more fish is being quick-frozen these days. There are now freezer-trawlers, fishing in distant waters, which freeze their catch whole. From super-market to village shop frozen fish is available all over the country. Consequently, any type of fish is available at any time of the year.

But for those who prefer to buy their fish fresh, here is a guide to fish in season.

Fish	*When in Season*
BASS	From May to December
BLOATERS	September to April
BREAM	All the year, but best and cheapest in autumn
CHUB	June to November. Best in summer
COCKLES	All the year
COD	October to April. Best in February and March
CRABS	April to October. Best in the summer
EELS	June to March. Best in autumn
FLOUNDERS	All the year. Best August to December
GRAYILNG	July to January
HADDOCK	All the year. Best in winter
HAKE	April to August. Best in early summer
HALIBUT	All the year

Fish	*When in Season*
HERRINGS	May to November
LOBSTERS	All the year, but best in summer
MACKEREL	March to July
MULLET	All the year. Best in summer
MUSSELS	All the year. Best in autumn and winter
OYSTERS	September to April. Best in winter
PERCH	May to January
PIKE	September to January
PLAICE	All the year
PRAWNS	All the year. Best May to December
SALMON	February to September
SCALLOPS	September to March
SHRIMPS	All the year. Best from April to November
SKATE	October to May
SMELTS	October to May
SOLES	All the year
SPRATS	November to March
STURGEON	April to September
TROUT	Freshwater trout April-September (Rainbow trout obtainable all the year)
TURBOT	All the year
WHITEBAIT	February to September
WHITING	All the year. Best in autumn and winter

Sauces

Basic White Sauce (Sauce Béchamel)

½ pint milk
1½ oz butter
2 level tabs. plain flour

Very low heat is needed for cooking this basic sauce. Use a double saucepan or one with a thick bottom.

Melt the butter until it begins to foam. Remove from heat and add the flour. Stir well. Pour in a little of the milk, previously warmed. Put back upon the low heat, stirring steadily to form a thick paste free from lumps. Gradually add the remainder of the warm milk, still stirring. Season with salt, pepper, and a little nutmeg, if liked.

Let the sauce simmer very gently *for at least 10 minutes*, stirring constantly.

If, by any evil chance, lumps have formed, all is not lost. Sieve it into a clean saucepan, or put it into the electric liquidizer, and reheat. The best way to keep Béchamel sauce hot, and also to give it time to mature properly, is to use a bain-marie, but the double saucepan is the next best thing.

Sauce Béchamel can be made with white stock instead of milk, in which case its correct name is *Béchamel grasse*.

An infinite variety of sauces can be made from about ½ pint basic white sauce. Here are some of them:

Anchovy

Add 1 tab. anchovy essence and a squeeze of lemon juice. (For fish dishes.)

Caper

Add 2 tabs. chopped capers and 1 tab. of caper vinegar. (For boiled mutton, mackerel and herring.)

Celery

Add a purée of celery, and a little cream. (For boiled chicken, pheasant and partridge.)

Cheese (Sauce Mornay)

Add 2 heaped tabs. of grated Parmesan or Gruyère cheese. Don't let this sauce cook too long. The cheese should *just* melt. The yolk of an egg, added finally, improves this useful sauce. (Fish, chicken, spinach, eggs, etc.)

Cucumber

Add 4 tabs. grated and peeled cucumber and a pinch of nutmeg. (For fish.)

Eggs

Add a generous amount of chopped hard-boiled eggs. (For boiled fish.)

Maître d'Hôtel

Add heaped tab. chopped parsley, a squeeze of lemon juice and yolk of one egg. (For fish and poultry.)

Mushroom

Add 2 oz chopped and lightly fried mushrooms.

Mustard

Mix 1 dessertsp. French mustard with the roux. An egg yolk, added finally, improves flavour and colour of this sauce. (For boiled beef, herring, mackerel, etc.)

Onion

Add well-chopped cooked onion and a small knob of butter with seasoning. (For roast mutton.)

can be added some 15 minutes before the dish is ready, or an egg yolk and cream *always added off the heat* and immediately before serving, gives thickness to the liquor.

(4) *Broths* which contain meat, cereals and vegetables, but have no additional thickening agent. It cannot be stressed too often that cereals such as rice and pearl barley, which are used in this class of soup, must be thoroughly washed and blanched before use in all soup recipes, otherwise cloudiness will result.

English people seem to prefer thick soups. Maybe our climate has something to do with this preference. But a bowl of well-made consommé is so particularly light and such a perfect beginning to a meal, either hot or cold, that I have given several suggestions in this section.

A little wine added to some soups can improve their flavour, and all soups need to be carefully checked for seasoning and tasted before serving. As a rough-and-ready rule allow 1 tab. of wine to 4 people. Clear soups will take Madeira, Marsala or a fruity sherry very happily. Game soups are improved with the same quantity of wine, but Burgundy or port may be substituted. Be discreet, rather than lavish, when adding wine to soup, or any other dish for that matter.

You will not find many cold soups in this book. Any that are here will be found in the Summer section with the exception of Vichyssoise, perhaps the most famous cold soup. It needs leeks which, as Elizabeth David points out, are unobtainable to English cooks in the summer when this dish is most suitable, but for those who are hardy enough to take iced Vichyssoise when leeks are in season, I include it under Autumn and hope that it will be a mild night when it is served.

Pot-au-feu

You are preparing two things here. The meat and vegetables will be served hot as one meal, and the beef broth will form the basis of future soups. A large stock-pot, saucepan or stew-pan will be needed.

3 lb lean beef. Shin, brisket
or silverside are suitable
1 lb knuckle of veal, including
bone
1 stick celery
1 onion
1 carrot

1 small turnip, but omit this
unless it is young
Herbs tied in muslin (parsley,
bayleaf, thyme, 1 dozen
peppercorns and 2 cloves)
Salt to taste
6 pints cold water

Put meat and bones with salt and water into the pan. Bring
to boil *very slowly*. Add a spoonful of cold water just before boiling
point to help scrum to rise. Skim well. Simmer gently for about
an hour, then add herbs and vegetables, peeled but left whole.
Continue simmering for a further 3 hours.

Remove meat and vegetables and serve hot, moistened with a
little of liquor. A dish of mashed potatoes or hot rice can accompany this dish.

Strain the liquor into a clean bowl and let it get cold. Remove
the fat. You now have a good beef *bouillon* for the making of
soups and gravies. For a really clear bright soup the stock may
need further clearing, and you may well feel that the additional
work, time and expense is not warranted. However, remember
that your finished consommé is an exceptionally fine, strong and
nutritious product and for those of you who wish to try it, here
is the classic method.

To clear the stock you will need:

½ lb lean beef, such as shin
2 pints of the stock
Whites and shells of 2 eggs
Seasoning

Mince the meat and soak in a teacupful of cold water for half
an hour. Put into a large saucepan, add stock from which all fat
has been removed, crushed egg shells, the whites, whisked to a
froth, and salt and pepper.

Heat, and stir briskly, until liquid boils. Allow it to boil rapidly
for 5 minutes, then lower heat and let it simmer for half an hour.
A thick scum will have risen. Remove this, and let the liquor
cool a little. Pour it through a wet cloth into a clean vessel.

This clear stock is the basis of all clear soups. The particular garnish gives the soup its name. The best known, perhaps, is:

Consommé Julienne

2 pints cleared stock	½ small turnip
1 leek	Pepper and salt
1 carrot	½ wine glass Madeira or
1 small onion	sherry, if desired

Chop all the vegetables into fine shreds about the size of a match-stick. Simmer in salted water until tender, about half an hour. Heat the stock separately, strain vegetables and add to the stock. Add the wine before serving.

This is just as delicious cold, when it should be in the form of a light jelly. A small cup of consommé, either hot or cold, will often be accepted by an invalid when other food is refused, and has been recognized for generations as a wonderful restorative.

Here are other ways of serving consommé.

Consommé with rice

2 pints cleared stock
1 oz rice, preferably Carolina or Patna
Seasoning

Wash rice thoroughly. Drop into plenty of boiling water and boil for 12 minutes or until the grains break easily. Drain, rinse and put in the warmed tureen to reheat. Pour on hot seasoned stock, and serve.

Consommé with batter threads

Small dessertsp. flour
1 egg
Pepper and salt
2 tabs. milk or thin cream

Beat ingredients together to form a light smooth batter. Heat the stock, and whilst heating pour in the batter and stir. It should boil for about 3 minutes, and the cooked batter will form fine threads permeating the soup. Serve very hot.

Consommé with mushrooms

¼ lb small button mushrooms
2 pints clear stock
1 oz butter
Tablespoon of sherry
Seasoning

Melt butter in a saucepan. Simmer finely sliced mushrooms in the butter for about 5 minutes. Add the stock and bring to the boil. Check seasoning before adding sherry and serve very hot.

Grated Parmesan or Gruyère cheese is good with most clear soups.

Basic Fish Soup

English people tend to look upon fish soup with some suspicion. It does seem wrong, though, to throw away some delicious liquor in which a large piece of fish has been boiled. It will form the base of many interesting soups.

Let the stock get cold and then strain it.

2 pints of prepared stock
1 onion
½ lb of any type of cooked fish
1 oz flour

1 oz butter
A little chopped parsley
Salt and pepper
½ pint milk

Bring stock to boiling point. Add chopped onion and simmer till soft. Strain. Mix flour with a little milk, add the rest of the milk and stir into the stock. Let it boil. Cook for 10 minutes, add seasoning and flaked fish. Finally add parsley and butter. Serve very hot.

There are many variations of this basic soup.

Shelled shrimps, fragments of crab or lobster, or chopped watercress can be added.

An ounce of sago added to the stock half an hour or so before the flavourings are added, thickens the soup beautifully.

Hors d'oeuvre

Hors d'oeuvre, starters, appetizers, call them what you will, but the aim of this first course remains the same. It is to arouse your interest in the meal. It should appeal to the eye and sometimes, the nose, as well as the palate.

It need not be an expensive affair. It need not involve a plethora of dishes. What could be simpler than a shrimp-stuffed egg or finely-sliced sweet peppers? It can be one such delicacy served individually, put in place when the table is set, or a number of complementary dishes arranged as an attractive centre-piece on the table. If you are preparing a multiple hors d'oeuvre it is as well to keep in mind Mrs Elizabeth David's wise advice.

'I would say that a well composed mixed hors d'oeuvre consists, approximately, of something raw, something salt, something dry or meaty, something gentle and smooth, and possibly something in the way of fresh fish. Simplified though it is, a choice based roughly on these lines won't be far wrong.'

You will find recipes to cover all these categories in the hors d'oeuvre sections of this book.

Some of the dishes may well be used as the main course; for instance, some of the egg dishes and the savoury open tarts such as Quiche Lorraine.

Stuffed Eggs

The advantage of hard-boiled eggs is that they lend themselves to a wide variety of stuffings and always look attractive.

Hard-boil (8 or 9 minutes) an egg for each person. Cut in half lengthwise and remove yolk. Mix the yolk with any of these suggested ingredients:

Cream cheese, mashed sardines, chopped shrimps, a little softened butter with curry powder, or anchovy sauce. Finely chopped celery or celery salt goes well with the cream cheese filling. A little paprika decorates prettily, and the eggs should be served either on a round of brown bread and butter, or a bed of mustard and cress.

Eggs Mimosa

This is a rather dressy version of stuffed eggs – but a real eye-catcher.

Scoop out the yolk of hard-boiled egg – one per person is enough – and set aside. Fill cavity with a well-flavoured stuffing such as pâté or shrimps pounded with anchovy sauce, and put halves together again. Cover lightly with a good white sauce or a little mayonnaise.

Now sieve the egg-yolks coarsely and roll the eggs in them so that they are thickly covered with yellow fluff.

Serve with sprigs of greenery and quartered tomatoes.

Scotch Eggs

Hard-boiled eggs
2 oz sausage meat for each egg
Oil for frying
Breadcrumbs and beaten egg

Peel the hard-boiled eggs and roll in flour. Wrap each in fairly thin sausage meat, but do not stretch the latter or it will disintegrate in cooking.

Roll in beaten egg, then breadcrumbs and fry in deep fat until brown. Cut in half when cold, and serve with watercress or lettuce.

Scotch eggs, of course, are equally good served hot with suitable vegetables. Hot tomatoes, puréed, are especially attractive.

Potted Shrimps

These are cheaper and nicer if you make them yourself, and are extremely simple. Buy shrimps already peeled.

> 1 lb or pint of peeled shrimps
> 3 oz butter
> Pinch of nutmeg and pepper

Heat the butter and keep a little aside. Stir in the shrimps, nutmeg and pepper. When thoroughly coated with the butter, put the mixture into little pots, and pour a layer of melted butter on top. Chill.

When needed, serve with brown bread and butter and a wedge of lemon.

Crab and lobster meat or prawns can be treated successfully by the same method.

Scotch Woodcock

This is a hot savoury which seems to have fallen out of favour these days. It makes a splendid starter, particularly if the main dish is a cold one.

Butter toast and spread with anchovy paste, or a little anchovy sauce. Scramble eggs – one per person (and for pity's sake use butter and NEVER, repeat NEVER, so much as a spot of milk or you will get that ghastly boiled-blanket taste, and serve you right!).

Spread eggs thickly on the toast, criss-cross them with two anchovy fillets, and put a slice of tomato or olive as decoration.

Men, particularly, relish this dish.

Devils on Horseback

2 rashers per person. Streaky is best.
Chicken liver
Chopped shallot and parsley
Cayenne pepper

Wrap a small portion of chicken liver in each rasher, having first sprinkled it with the chopped shallot, parsley and a little shaking of cayenne. Grill, and when sizzling mount on toast and serve immediately.

There are also *Angels on Horseback*, and for these use oysters instead of the chicken liver, and omit the shallot, parsley and pepper.

Bacon and Egg Tart
(Quiche Lorraine)

Pastry:

6 oz flour   Pinch of salt
3 oz butter   Water to mix

Filling:

4 rashers of bacon	½ pint thin cream
2 eggs	Salt and pepper

Make the short pastry 2 or 3 hours before using and leave it in a cool place.

Butter a flat pie-tin. Roll out the pastry and line the tin.

Melt some butter in a saucepan or frying-pan, and cook the rashers, first cutting them into small pieces, until they are softened. Remove and put on the pastry. Beat together eggs, cream, salt and pepper. Pour into pastry case, and bake in a hot oven for 30 minutes. Serve whilst still warm.

Equally good fillings are:

(1) ½ lb mushrooms	Gill of thin cream
1 onion	2 oz butter
2 rashers of bacon	Salt and pepper

Cook sliced onion, mushrooms and chopped rashers in the melted butter, until soft. Drain off surplus butter. Pour the cream into the mixture, season, and then put filling in the tart case. Bake in a moderate oven for 30 minutes. If you put a pastry lid on this tart, then allow 5 or 10 minutes longer for cooking.

(2) Cooked asparagus tips in cheese sauce. In this case, the pastry should be 'baked blind' first, as the asparagus filling will take only a short time to cook.

Cheese Soufflé

2 oz butter	½ pint milk
2 oz flour	2 yolks and 4 whites of egg
2 oz grated cheese	Pepper and salt

Melt the butter in a saucepan, add the flour as for a roux, and gradually add the milk, stirring the while until it thickens. Remove from heat and add all the other ingredients, except the 4 whites of egg. Mix well together. Whip whites stiffly and fold into mixture.

Bake for 30 minutes in a hot oven, and serve immediately.

Cheese Aigrettes

2 oz flour
2 oz cheese
1 oz butter

2 eggs
1 gill water
Pepper and salt

Put butter and water in a saucepan and bring to the boil. Shake in flour very gradually, stirring continuously. When the mixture begins to come away from the sides add the grated cheese, continuing to stir. Let it cool slightly. Beat in the eggs and seasoning until smooth.

Have ready a pan of boiling fat. Drop in spoonfuls of the mixture, and cook until golden brown. Drain well, and sprinkle with a little grated cheese and cayenne pepper. Serve very hot.

This dish, served with a green salad, makes a pleasant main course.

Cheese and Egg Toast

2 hard-boiled eggs
2 oz grated cheese
1 oz butter
Slices of toast

Remove yolks and pound with the butter and cheese. Season well with cayenne, salt and mustard. Spread the mixture on hot toast, and brown under the grill.

Kedgeree

½ lb salted smoked Finnan haddock
2 oz butter
2 tabs. cream
2 hard boiled eggs
2 tabs. rice

Put rice in saucepan of boiling salted water, and haddock into another with unsalted water. Cook both for about 10–12 minutes. Strain the rice and the fish. Flake the latter.

Melt the butter and turn fish and rice into it. Mix well. Add the cream. Remove egg yolks, chop up the whites and add to the mixture. Serve very hot, garnished with a little parsley and the sliced egg yolks, and with hot toast.

This is a fairly substantial dish and should be followed by something light and cold – ham mousse, for instance – or it would make a good main dish.

Kromeskis

These are lovely little savoury fritters, and as they must be served very hot and are quite filling, they are best followed by a light cold dish.

Partly fry strips of fat bacon, each about 3 in. by 1½ in. In the centre of each place a teaspoonful of minced fish, shellfish or meat, well-seasoned with appropriate herbs and moistened with beaten egg-yolk to bind. Roll up the stuffed pieces of bacon, allow them to cool, then dip into batter and fry to a golden brown. Pile on a dish and serve piping hot.

Eggs

Eggs are at their most plentiful in spring and low in price. There are a number of egg recipes included in the hors d'oeuvre sections, some of which are quite substantial enough for a main course. However, here are one or two more which you may enjoy.

Curried Buttered Eggs

For 4 helpings you will need:

4 hard-boiled eggs	Crisp breadcrumbs
2 raw eggs	½ tsp. curry powder
1 oz butter	Salt and cayenne pepper

Butter a fireproof dish, slice the hard-boiled eggs and arrange them in the dish. Sprinkle with curry powder and a shake of cayenne pepper and salt.

Beat the raw eggs and pour over the hard-boiled ones. Sprinkle with breadcrumbs, dot plentifully with butter and bake for 10–15 minutes in a fairly hot oven.

Eggs with Ham

4 eggs	2 tabs. crips breadcrumbs
2 oz finely chopped cooked ham	1 tsp. chopped chives, basil or parsley
Mushroom ketchup or tomato purée	Salt and pepper
2 tabs. white sauce or brown gravy	

Butter 4 ramekins. Mix ham, ketchup or purée with salt, pepper and selected herbs. Moisten with white sauce or gravy, to a nice squashiness. Put the mixture at the bottom of the ramekins.

Break an egg carefully into each little dish. Sprinkle with breadcrumbs and butter. They will take about 10-15 minutes in the middle of a moderate oven.

Fluffy Omelette

Although one has the same ingredients for this type of omelette as for the usual variety, it looks far more exotic and lends itself to dozens of different accompaniments, such as ham, spinach, mushroom, tomato, shrimp or simply fresh herbs from the garden.

Don't forget, too, that a sweet omelette is delicious. Served with a hot sauce made from home-made jam diluted slightly with a spoonful or two of water and lemon-juice, this a simple and sustaining sweet.

For each person you will need:

> 2 eggs
> 1 tab. water
> Pinch of salt and pepper
> (or ½ tsp. of sugar if you are making
> a sweet omelette)

Separate the whites from the yolks, and beat the whites until they are stiff. Beat the yolks, season, add the spoonful of water and beat again.

Butter an omelette pan or frying pan, and heat it until it begins to sizzle.

Now fold in the stiffly beaten whites and pour the mixture into the pan. As this method makes a thick omelette, you may need to put your pan under a hot grill to brown the top. This should be ready while the omelette is cooking so that the whole operation is speedily done. Serve immediately.

Poached eggs are a great standby and are delicious served on sliced ham, tongue, a bed of spinach, curried rice or spaghetti, vermicelli, etc., in tomato or cheese sauce. Don't be afraid to trim them with the kitchen scissors to a neat shape if they have spread themselves during cooking. A sprinkling of paprika, or chopped parsley or chives, improves the look of a poached egg.

Main Dishes

Cod Cutlets in Cider

4 cod cutlets (or fillets)	1 lemon
2 onions	Browned breadcrumbs
Chopped parsley	½ oz butter
	½ pint cider

Slice one onion and arrange at the bottom of a greased fire-proof dish. Peel the lemon and slice it finely, putting half with the onion and a sprinkling of parsley, salt and pepper.

Now arrange the cutlets on top. Put the rest of the mixture of onions, lemon slices and parsley over them. Just cover with the cider, and sprinkle top with breadcrumbs. Dot with the butter and cook in a moderate oven for about 30–40 minutes.

Soles

The Dover sole is the true sole, but the lemon sole is the one more often encountered, and very much cheaper. Both are in season all the year round and are obliging enough to come in all sizes. Another advantage of soles is their ability to stay fresh longer than any other fish. Soles also rank second only to whiting for digestibility. Furthermore, they lend themselves happily to all manner of cooking methods, and according to one cook there are at least sixty ways of dressing these useful fish.

I do not intend to give you such well-known recipes as Fried Sole, Fillets of Sole Bonne Femme or Fillets of Sole Meunière for, no doubt, these are in your cookery books already. But here are one or two ways of cooking sole which you may like to try.

The first is a recipe from Eliza Acton's *Modern Cookery for Private Families* (1845).

Soles au plat

'Clarify from two to three ounces of fresh butter, and pour it into the dish in which the fish are to be served; add to it a little salt, some cayenne, and teaspoonful of essence of anchovies, and from one to two glasses of sherry, or any other dry white wine; lay in a couple of fine soles which have been well cleaned and wiped very dry, strew over them a thick layer of fine bread-crumbs, moisten them with clarified butter, set the dish in a moderate oven, and bake the fish for a quarter of an hour. A layer of shrimps placed between the soles is a great improvement; and we would also recommend a little lemon juice to be mixed with the sauce.

Baked, 15 minutes.

Obs: The soles, we think, better without the wine in this receipt. They require but a small portion of liquid, which might be supplied by a little additional butter, a spoonful of water or pale gravy, the lemon-juice, and store-sauce. Minced parsley may be mixed with the bread-crumbs when it is liked.'

Venetian Fillets of Sole

Allow a good-sized sole fillet per person	2 tabs. chopped parsley
	½ pint Tartare Sauce
1 oz butter	2 finely-chopped shallots
1 large tomato	Pepper and salt

Bake the fillets slowly in a covered dish, first arranging sliced tomatoes, chopped shallots and parsley neatly along each.

When they are done, which will take about 20 minutes, pour round them the Tartare Sauce made as follows:

Melt 1 oz butter. Add 1 oz minced onion and 1 dessertsp. chopped parsley, and a tiny flake or two of garlic. Cook until golden brown, then add a wine-glass each of wine-vinegar and stock (water, if there is no stock available) a pinch of salt and a pinch of white sugar. Simmer for a few minutes, then strain.

This dish looks most decorative if the Tartare Sauce is coloured green by the addition of liquid obtained from cooking spinach in a small amount of water.

Chopped mushrooms, gherkins or capers should be added at the end of the sauce-making.

Sole in Pastry

4 fillets of sole	4 oz mushrooms
¾ lb rough puff pastry	Juice of 1 lemon
1 egg for glazing	Salt and pepper

Roll pastry thinly into a large square, and divide into 4. Put a fillet on each, crosswise, and sprinkle with lemon juice, salt and pepper.

Chop the mushrooms and put on top. Fold pastry over fish to make a triangular shape. Seal the edges with a little of the beaten egg. Brush the top with the rest, and set to bake in a fairly hot oven for about 20 minutes.

Cooked tomatoes, spinach, or sweet corn are all good with this dish, or a fresh salad, if preferred.

Soles lend themselves very well to paper-bag cookery, *en papillotes* as you will see it in most cookery books. Paper cases made to enclose small portions of fish or meat, sometimes partly cooked beforehand, ensure that the juices of the cutlet or fillet so cooked will be preserved. Nowadays, we sometimes prefer to wrap our pieces in aluminium foil.

The finished product is not only extremely tasty and tender, but the oven is kept clean, no smells emerge and the little parcel looks rather exciting on the plate.

Sole en Papillotes

This recipe can equally well be used for fillets of plaice, halibut, cod, etc.

Allow a good-sized fillet for each person. Sprinkle with a little lemon juice, salt and pepper, and place in a piece of buttered aluminium foil or greaseproof paper.

Fold the ends securely, and bake for 15 minutes, or longer, according to the size and thickness of the fillets.

Delicious additions such as partly cooked mushrooms, tomatoes or onions can be put inside the case with the fish.

Open the parcel a little when serving so that the aroma can emerge, the juices are still comfortably held, and the eater can open it more easily at the table.

If you are *frying fillets of sole,* or any other fillets, try rolling them. Wash and dry the fillets, sprinkle with salt, pepper, chopped parsley and lemon juice, then roll them up and fasten with a wooden cherry stick.

Dip in beaten egg and then breadcrumbs and fry in deep fat in the usual way. Drain well, remove sticks, and make a neat arrangement of the rolls on a hot serving dish. Garnish with lemon slices and parsley. A dish of fried rolled fillets looks more attractive than flat fillets and they take up less room on the serving dish.

Halibut and Turbot

Both fish are available throughout the year, but halibut is at its best in Spring and turbot from March until September. They are both splendidly large fish, with firm white flesh of a delicious flavour.

Occasionally, a *Whole Boiled Turbot* is still served for a dinner party. This is the method of cooking it.

Soak the fish in salted water for 2-3 hours. Clean well, but do not remove the fins. Place the fish in a large vessel – a fish kettle if you are lucky enough to have one – cover with salted water and allow it to simmer gently.

Allow about half an hour's simmering. As soon as the flesh comes easily from the bone it is done. Lift out the turbot and drain well.

Serve garnished with lemon wedges and parsley. Shrimp sauce is the usual accompaniment to this noble dish.

Cuts of turbot are more usually bought than the whole fish when only a few are to be served. Here is a simple way of cooking a piece of turbot to supply a dish for 4 people.

Turbot with Tomatoes

1½ lb of turbot in the piece
Two large tomatoes
1 oz butter

Salt, pepper and chopped parsley
Small cupful water or fish-stock

Wash the fish and put it in a casserole with water or fish stock. Dot with butter. Cover and cook in a moderate oven for 15–20 minutes.

Pour off the liquid into a saucepan. Add the chopped tomatoes, salt and pepper. Simmer for 5 minutes, sieve, and pour the sauce over the hot turbot. Serve at once, sprinkled with the chopped parsley.

Turbot with Aubergines

4 turbot steaks
1 large aubergine
Juice of ½ lemon

2 tabs. tomato purée
¼ pint fish stock
3 tabs. cream
2 tabs. olive oil

Sprinkle the steaks with lemon juice, salt and pepper. Place in fireproof casserole with a cupful of water. Cook gently, covered, for 20 minutes.

Meanwhile, slice the aubergine, soak for 5 minutes in salted water, remove, and pat the slices dry.

Heat the olive oil in a frying-pan. Cook the aubergine slices until brown. Add tomato purée, pour off fish stock from the cooked steaks and add to the frying-pan, stirring the while. Season to taste.

Place the aubergine neatly on the steaks. Now add the cream to the tomato sauce, making sure that the pan has first been removed from the heat. Blend well and pour over the steaks. Serve at once.

Halibut can be substituted for turbot in these last two recipes very satisfactorily.

Halibut au Gratin

4 halibut steaks	1 egg
1 oz butter	2 tabs. toasted breadcrumbs
1 small onion	3 tabs. single cream
¼ lb mushrooms	1 tsp. lemon juice
	Salt and pepper

Put finely chopped onion and mushrooms into a fireproof dish and arrange steaks on this bed, first coating them with egg and breadcrumbs.

Sprinkle with lemon juice and seasoning. Add the thin cream, dot with butter, and bake in a slow oven for 45–50 minutes.

Watercress makes a nice garnish for this dish.

Halibut Pie

2 lb halibut	1 raw egg
1 small onion	Basil, chives and parsley
2 oz butter	Pepper and salt
2 hard-boiled eggs	Flaky pastry to cover

Parboil the halibut, with the onion, and remove the flesh. Put this in a greased pie-dish, with the onion finely chopped. Sprinkle with finely chopped basil, chives and parsley. If liked, fennel can be substituted for these herbs.

Strain and thicken the fish liquor with butter and flour. Moisten the ingredients of the pie dish with this sauce. Slice the hard-boiled eggs, and place them on top, dotted with a little butter.

Cover with flaky pastry. Brush this with beaten egg-yolk to gild it, and bake in a brisk oven for 30 minutes.

Both halibut and turbot steaks or collops (i.e. neat shapes) are excellent fried in deep fat, oil preferably. Simply wash and dry your pieces, dredge with seasoned flour, dip in beaten egg and then breadcrumb them and immerse in hot fat from which a faint blue smoke is rising. Remember with these two firm-fleshed fishes, that they will take longer to cook than, say, plaice.

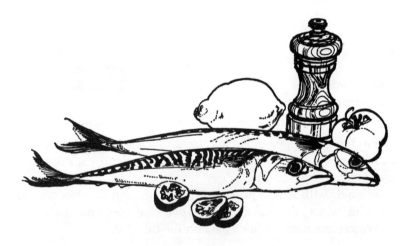

Baked Mackerel

Mackerel, like herrings, are rich in natural fat – too rich for some people's taste, in fact. Here is an agreeable method of cooking them which makes them easier to digest.

1 mackerel per person
2 lemons
2 large tomatoes
1 oz butter
Salt and pepper

Cut off heads and clean the mackerel. Sprinkle with salt and pepper. Butter some foil, a good-sized piece for each fish, and place each of the mackerel upon its piece.

Slice the lemons and tomatoes and arrange alternately along the length of the fish. Dot with butter, fold and seal the foil, and place the parcels in a fireproof dish to bake.

They will need 30–40 minutes in a slow to moderate oven. Remove foil, and serve, very hot, with their cooking juices about them.

Grilled Cod with Cheese

4 cutlets, steaks or fillets, about one
inch thick
1 oz butter
2 oz grated cheese
Salt and pepper

Grease a grill pan and put in the cutlets. Grill, on one side only, for about 3–4 minutes. Turn the fish over and remove from heat.

Cream butter, cheese, salt and pepper together and spread the uncooked side of the fish, thickly and evenly. Return the grill pan to a slightly lower heat and cook gently until fish is done and the coating is browned. This should take about 10 minutes.

Serve at once. A sprinkling of paprika improves the look of these grilled cutlets.

Hashed Cod

1½ lb cooked cod   1 oz butter
¼ pint prepared shrimps   1 oz flour
1 pint milk   Seasoning

Flake the cod. Blend flour into melted butter, add milk to make a white sauce, stirring as it thickens. Add the shrimps, the flaked cod and seasoning. Cook until thoroughly heated.

Serve with a border of mashed potato. A pinch of grated nut-meg and a well-beaten egg added to the potatoes gives them added attraction. A little fresh-chopped parsley, or a dusting of paprika, finishes this dish very prettily.

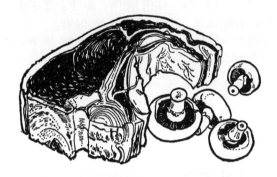

Mrs Beeton's splendid *Book of Household Management* first came out in monthly parts during the period 1859–1861, some four-teen years, you may observe, after Eliza Acton's *Modern Cookery for Private Families* was published.

Recipes apart, she is worth reading for her reverberating paragraphs. I like particularly the introduction to the meat dishes which is headed 'General Observations on Quadrupeds' and opens with this arresting sentence.

'By the general assent of Mankind, the Empire of Nature has been divided into three kingdoms'; and after several pages of accurate and detailed matter she arrives at this point, where we are happy to join her:

'Many animals', she remarks, 'are injurious to man, but most of them, in some shape or other, he turns to his service. Of these there is none he has made more subservient than the common ox, of which there is scarcely a part that he has not been able to con-vert into some useful purpose.'

She goes on to list the articles made from the horns, hide, sinews, blood, bone and hair. I can't help feeling that she is stretching things a bit when she tells us solemnly that 'their blood is made the basis of Prussian blue'. Perhaps there is some weightier purpose for Prussian blue than forming one of the squares in a child's paint-box. I feel sure that there must be, or Isabella would not have brought it to our notice.

After that, there is a fascinating description of various breeds, and in my facsimile edition, published in 1968, there are some lovely pictures of oxen, before arriving at some score of pages devoted to beef recipes.

Nowadays, of course, beef is the most expensive meat (with the exception of veal) to be had, so that some of the recipes, so economical in 1860, are now extravagant. Here is one of Mrs Beeton's, which I give because it is a simple and unusual way of cooking beef. Mrs Beeton says 'rump-steaks', but you could make a good dish from a less expensive cut, marinaded for a few hours in 4 parts of olive oil to 1 part of wine vinegar.

Baked Beef-Steak Pudding

Ingredients: 6 oz flour, 2 eggs, not quite 1 pint of milk, salt to taste, 1½ lbs rump-steaks, 1 kidney, pepper and salt.

Mode: Cut the steaks into nice square pieces, with a small quantity of fat, and the kidney divide into small pieces.

Make a batter of flour, eggs and milk in the above proportion; lay a little of it at the bottom of a pie-dish; then put in the steaks and kidney, which should be well seasoned with pepper and salt, and pour over the remainder of the batter, and bake for 1½ hours in a brisk but not fierce oven.

Time: 1½ hour   *Average cost:* 2s. (Ah me!)

Sufficient for 4 or 5 persons

Seasonable at any time.'

Here is a modern method of cooking steak for those who have a fondue set to use. You will need *for each person:*

4–6 oz fillet or tender rump steak

8–10 pineapple cubes

Cut steak into bite-sized pieces, and chop the pineapple cubes in half. Arrange on individual plates with the fondue forks or skewers in readiness.

Fill the fondue container about half or two-thirds full of vegetable oil. Make the oil very hot.

Guests spear a cube of meat and a half-cube of pineapple together and sizzle it to their liking.

A bowl of green salad, and crisps, or French bread, should be served with the fondue.

Steaks

There are so many terms used these days when referring to beef steaks that it might be helpful to give a brief explanation. I don't think that I can do better than quote the 1960 edition of Mrs Beeton which gives the following up-to-date descriptions:

'*Fillet*: This term is used in two ways. Correctly it refers to the meat found beneath the blade part of the loin bones. It is also used for the continuation of this same muscle which is part of a whole unboned rump steak or steak piece. This part is properly called *the undercut*. Fillet or undercut may be served in several ways and under several names.

Chateaubriand: A very thick piece of fillet sufficient for two people and cut at the time of serving into two portions.

Tournedos: Thick slices of fillet for one person. Usually ¾ inch thick and a nice round shape, they are perhaps the most usual way in which the steak is cooked.

Noisettes: Neatly trimmed, round or oval shapes of fillet between ½ and ¾ inch thick.

Mignons: Very fine fillet steak which should be cooked quickly. These are often referred to as *minute steaks*.

Porterhouse: A steak from the wing end (wing rib) of the sirloin or forerib. In fact a slice from the part of the loin which contains no undercut or fillet.

T-bone steak: A steak cut through the sirloin so that it contains on one side at least, the T-shaped loin bone. It has two "eyes", that of the loin meat and that of the fillet.

Entrecôte: This is a sirloin steak without the undercut and without the bone. In other words, the eye meat of the loin cut into steaks.

All these steaks may be served in many different ways. For example, an ordinary Chateaubriand is dipped in olive oil, salted, peppered and grilled. Garnished with hearts of artichoke, stuffed braised lettuce and Maître d'Hôtel butter it becomes *Chateaubriand Marquise.* If you sauté a sirloin steak with mushrooms and shallots in butter, and then make a sauce of the vegetables with dry white wine and thick gravy it is an *Entrecôte Forestière.* With *red wine* instead of white and marrowbone cooked in the sauce it becomes *Entrecôte Bordelaise.*

A mignon or minute steak cooked quickly in butter with a little Worcester sauce and chopped parsley is a *Boeuf Minute Diane.*

The methods of cooking tournedos are legion. For example, *Tournedos Andalouse* is served with grilled tomatoes on buttered toast garnished with aubergines, small onions and Madeira sauce. Cooked in butter and served with a sauce of tomatoes, mushrooms and shallots poured over the top they become *Tournedos Chasseur.*

There are indeed more ways to cook steak than in the frying pan.'

And it is for this reason that I have quoted so fully from this excellent and concise entry in a modern *Cookery and Household Management* by Mrs Beeton. Steak today is so very expensive that one cannot afford a culinary disaster. Study the cuts carefully, consult your butcher, and follow your chosen recipe faithfully to get good results.

Using up Cold Beef

The residue of a good joint of sirloin, topside or rib, lends itself to many attractive dishes. Most of them involve the use of a mincer, but here is one which does not. As in all made-up dishes, it is the sauces, garnishes and piquant ingredients that give the dish its distinction. This recipe is for:

Old-fashioned Hash

Cut the cooked meat into neat cubes with 2 or 3 rashes of bacon.
Brown them in a little butter.

Thicken the butter with a tab. of flour, and season with salt,
cayenne pepper and nutmeg. Add stock to make about a pint
of gravy. Cover the meat with this and reheat. A little mushroom
ketchup gives this dish a nice tang.

Fricassees are another good way of using up cold beef. The
meat should be cut into small cubes and heated in a good sauce,
as shown in Fricassee of Rabbit.

Rissoles seem to have gone out of fashion, but they are excellent if made carefully. Mince the remains of the meat finely,
removing excess fat *and all gristle*. (Nothing is worse than en-
countering some ghastly cartilaginous lump in a dish like this.
What to do with it? Remove it from one's mouth, thus revolting
fellow-diners and heaping ignominy on your hostess, or swallow
it and pay the penalty?)

Moisten the mince with a little sauce or gravy and bind with a
beaten egg. Basil, curry powder, a little finely chopped thyme
or parsley can be added for flavouring.

Shape into little balls or pats, dip in egg and breadcrumbs and
fry quickly in deep fat.

Kromeskis can be made with well-flavoured minced beef
instead of fish. You will find the recipe for Kromeskis in the
index.

Savoury Pancakes, using minced beef, suitably flavoured, as a
filling, are always delicious.

Plain *Mince*, at which our spirits quailed when at school, can
be really appetizing, but the dish does need to be attractively
garnished. For pity's sake mince the cold beef *finely* – twice, if
you can bear it – taking out all gristle carefully. Be adventurous
with ingredients. The gravy will be a good strong one, of course,
but be careful not to have the consistency of the finished dish too
runny.

Consult your herb chart or try adding some chopped lightly-
fried mushrooms or onions, some minced olives, or some washed

sultanas. Little rolls or crisp bacon, triangles of fresh toast or fried bread make the dish look attractive, and poached eggs, one for each person, enliven the appearance of the mince, as well as adding nourishment.

Beef Olives can be made with cooked lean beef as I have explained in the recipe given for uncooked beef, but remember that these will need slower and longer cooking to bring out the flavour.

Cottage Pie is, without doubt, my favourite method of using up cold beef.

Mince the meat very finely, with 2 rashers, freshly ground black pepper and a little salt added.

Lightly fry a small sliced onion, chop it and put through the mincer with the meat. Moisten well with beef gravy. Put into a greased pie-dish.

Cover with a lid – not too thick – of mashed potatoes made creamy with a knob of butter and an egg beaten into them. Add a pinch of nutmeg to the potatoes to bring out the flavour.

Cook in a moderate oven for about three quarters of an hour or a little longer depending on the size of the pie. Make sure that the top is nicely browned.

Curried Beef, of course, is excellent. It is usually made with minced beef, but here is a recipe from a favourite cookery book of mine called *Cunning Cookery* by Geoffrey Boumphrey. The recipe he gives is for chicken, but he points out that other meat is equally good served in this sauce.

'Make ½ pint of milk of coconut or almonds by infusing a breakfastcupful of shredded fresh (or dessicated) coconut, or half the quantity of ground sweet almonds, in boiling water for ½ hour – as tea is made, but for longer.

Fry 2 onions or 6 shallots, sliced, and a clove of garlic, finely chopped, in 2 oz butter until they begin to take colour. Stir in 2 tabs. of curry powder and cook the resultant paste for 2 or 3 mins.

Strain in half the milk and ½ pint of good stock, little by little, working out all the lumps, and leave the sauce to keep hot in a double-pan or *en bain-marie*.

Sauté the pieces of meat in some butter with a sliced shallot or two. Put them into the curry sauce, add a bay-leaf and the following ingredients – more or less ad lib: red currant jelly, chutney, a little of the coconut shreds or ground almonds, a little mixed spice and grated green ginger or ground ginger, slices of apple or currants – and leave it to keep hot for ½ hour or longer.

Strain in the rest of the coconut milk and the juice of half a lemon. Taste the sauce, and add more of any ingredient or not as seems best, and thicken with a little flour if necessary – reduce by evaporation if a dry curry is wanted. Serve with boiled rice.

Have one or more kinds of chutney handed round – and, if you have them, Bombay ducks, crisped in the oven.'

I have quoted this in full, for although you may not want to go to such trouble, this is a recipe which teems with ideas, and fairly bubbles with enthusiasm. It would certainly transform plain cold beef into something exotic.

The next two recipes are for Italian dishes. They are great favourites with those of us who go to the theatre at Oxford and emerge late from the Playhouse or the New in search of good food. At one Italian restaurant, in particular, one can count on welcoming smiles, no matter how advanced the hour, and either of these delicious dishes to comfort one. I hasten to add that these are only two from a bountiful menu.

Lasagne

You can buy a 1 lb box of the prepared pasta at any first-class grocer's. You will get about 2 dozen or so sheets of pasta, each about 4 in. by 4 in., made from durum wheat and eggs. For 4 people:

4–6 oz pasta	½ lb fresh tomatoes or 1 small
8–12 oz minced beef	tin of peeled Italian tomatoes
4 oz Gruyère or Cheddar	1 oz butter
cheese	1 small onion
2 tabs. Parmesan cheese	4 mushrooms

Cook pasta in salted water for 20 minutes or more. Drain,

rinse in cold water, drain again and pat dry with kitchen paper.

Make the filling by frying chopped onion and mushroom in the butter, adding the tomatoes, a little stock and minced beef. Season well, and cook for 10 minutes.

Arrange the pasta sheets in a greased dish, with alternate layers of filling, pasta and sliced cheese. Sprinkle with Parmesan cheese and bake in a fairly hot oven for 20–30 minutes.

Cannelloni Stuffed (though not with beef, but I want you to try this recipe.)

This can be made from the same pasta sheets, cooked as before.

Make a Béchamel sauce and add $\frac{1}{4}$ lb chopped mushrooms, lightly cooked in butter, to half of it.

Take the cooked sheets, drained and dried, and put a table-spoonful of filling upon each, roll up and place, crack side down, on a greased dish. Pour over the rest of the sauce, sprinkle well with Parmesan cheese and bake in a fairly hot oven for 20 minutes.

You can buy *green lasagne*, if you prefer it. It is flavoured and coloured with spinach, and although I haven't used it, I imagine it would be very good indeed.

Potted Beef

This useful food will provide a cold meal, fillings for sandwiches, or a delicious relish spread on hot toast.

The recipe given for Potted Hare on pages 144-5 can be used with finely minced beef in place of game.

Minced cold beef also makes a good filling for *patties* or a *plate-pie*. Use short, rough puff or flaky pastry. Line a deep plate, or individual patty-tins, if preferred, with the pastry.

Moisten the minced beef with gravy, and flavour with partly cooked onion, tomato, mushrooms or herbs to taste. Fill the dish with the mixture, put on the lid, and bake in a moderate oven for about 30 minutes. Small patties will be done in a little under the half-hour. Plate-pies and patties are equally good hot or cold, and are useful, when cold, for picnics or daily lunch-tins.

Baked Potatoes with Beef Stuffing

Scrub and prick large potatoes, allowing one per person. Put in the oven and cook until soft. Split lengthwise, remove the inside and mix it with minced beef, a little butter, milk and made mustard or horse-radish sauce.

Return the mixture to the cases and reheat for about 15 minutes.

Blinde Vinken

This is a Dutch recipe, rather like our beef olives. For 4 people you will need:

4 thin slices of lean uncooked beef	4 gherkins
4 thin slices of lean uncooked pork	1 oz butter
	Salt and black pepper
	Flour for thickening and stock

Sprinkle the beef slices with a little salt and pepper. Cover each with a slice of pork and put a gherkin on the pork.

Roll up and secure with a cherry stick.

Brown the little rolls in melted butter. Remove, whilst you add flour and stock to make good gravy. Return the 'blind finches' to the pan and let them simmer for an hour. Excellent with onions, celery or any tasty vegetable.

Oxford John

This recipe is equally good with slices of raw veal or lamb. The meat cooks so quickly, 5 minutes is quite long enough, that it is as well to have your guests absolutely ready. The dish can be cooked in a chafing-dish or in a heavy frying-pan.

Simply carve the raw beef into slices, just as if you were carving a joint at the table.* Season each collop with salt, pepper and a little nutmeg or a pinch of finely ground thyme.

Melt about 1 oz of butter in the pan and heat until it foams. Add a dessertspoonful of lemon juice, and put in the collops. Turn frequently until well coloured. Add some gravy to the pan, and simmer all together for a minute.

Serve immediately with the gravy poured over the meat, and hand the creamed potatoes, and any other selected vegetable, separately.

Sweet Sour Pork

1 lb fillet of pork	1 tab. white wine
1 tab. Soy sauce	1 tab. flour
1 tsp. each salt and brown sugar	2 egg yolks
	Oil for deep frying

Flatten the pork until it is very thin by beating it. Cut into 1-in. squares, and lightly fry in melted oil. Mix together all the other ingredients, and add the drained squares of pork. Reheat the oil, and drop the batter-covered pork into this and fry until crisp. Keep hot.

* Rump steak or sirloin are the best cuts for this dish. The slices should be about a ¼ in. thick, 4 in. in diameter, and neat in shape.

Sweet Sour Sauce

2 tabs. tomato ketchup
½ tsp. Worcester sauce
1 red and 1 green pepper, de-seeded and chopped finely
1 clove of crushed garlic

Small tin of chopped pine-apple
1 oz caster sugar
1 dessertsp. cornflour
1 tab. oil

Mix together all the ingredients except the cornflour. Simmer them together for a few minutes, then thicken with the cornflour, stirring continuously. It should be ready in about 5 minutes from the time of adding the thickening. Pour over the fried pork and serve immediately.

Potted Pork

This is a useful method of using up the remains of cooked pork.

1 lb minced cooked pork
A little ham or cooked bacon
3 oz butter
Nutmeg, salt and black pepper

Put all the meat through the mincer *twice*. Pound together, with butter and seasoning. Press into small pots and seal with melted butter on top.

This is excellent for sandwich fillings or served on hot toast. With a green salad and hard-boiled egg it can provide a light luncheon dish.

Roast Pork Stuffed with Apricots

Fore end of pork is best for this dish. Order a piece about 4 lb in weight and get the butcher to bone and score it for you.

For the stuffing you will need:

4 oz dried apricots (soaked for 4 hours and drained)
4 oz soft breadcrumbs
1 small chopped onion

1 tab. fresh parsley   Salt and black pepper
1 tsp. dry mustard   1 oz butter
1 egg

Sauté the onion in the butter. Add the rest of the ingredients, and bind well with beaten egg.

Spread this mixture inside the meat's cavity, and tie the joint neatly.

Roast in a fairly hot oven, allowing a good 40 minutes to the pound, stuffed weight. Baste frequently.

Sliced Belly of Pork

Belly of pork is equally good fresh or salted, but one has to be fond of fat to relish it. One of its greatest advantages is its cheapness. Here is one method of cooking this meat.

1 lb salt or fresh belly of pork   4 oz crisped breadcrumbs
Rind of 1 lemon   1 tab. dry mustard
1 egg   Pepper and salt

Get the butcher to remove rib bones and slice the meat into slices about ½ in. thick.

Beat the egg ready for dipping. Mix breadcrumbs, grated lemon rind and mustard. Dip each pork slice into beaten egg, coat with seasoned breadcrumb mixture, and put the slices into a greased shallow fireproof dish.

Bake in a fairly hot oven for 50–60 minutes. The slices should be crisp. Drain surplus fat before serving. Young whole carrots, broad beans and purple sprouting broccoli go well with this dish.

I expect you have noticed these days the truly remarkable dearth of *mutton* and the equally remarkable profusion of *lamb*! There seems to be a feeling about that mutton is rather démodé, and that lamb is really the thing. The fact that saddle of mutton is probably the greatest glory that a well-bred and well-fed sheep can produce is often forgotten.

I will do my best to put 'lamb' wherever I mean just that, and 'mutton' wherever that is applicable. Obviously, many of the recipes can use either.

As before, I shall not give specific recipes for such traditional dishes as roast leg of lamb, for these are readily available, but I hope that you will try some of these which are a little different.

Boiled Mutton with Caper Sauce

2½–3 lb leg of mutton
6 carrots
2 young turnips
½ young swede
Salt

Put leg of mutton into a large saucepan with cold water. Bring slowly to the boil, removing scum. It should simmer for about an hour before adding salt, and the carrots, left whole, and the swede and turnips cut in quarters.

Simmer for a further hour, or until meat is tender. Reckon 25 minutes to the pound of meat, and allow 20–25 minutes over.

Serve with vegetables about it. Mashed potatoes are good with this, and the caper sauce (see Sauces) should be served separately. Some people like little suet dumplings. These should be cooked separately in salted water, and will need about 20–30 minutes' boiling.

Savoury Breast of Mutton

Breast of mutton is very cheap and nourishing, but many people find it too fat. Here is a method of cooking it which minimizes the fatness, and produces a dish which is equally good hot or cold.

1 breast of mutton	Bouquet garni
2 sheep's tongues	Stick of celery
¼ lb lean ham	Hambone or bacon rinds
3 shallots	1 tsp. chopped tarragon or
Salt and pepper	thyme and 1 of parsley

Trim off excess fat from breast, and sprinkle with chopped herbs, pepper and salt.

Slice the partly-cooked sheep's tongues (or tinned ones do very well) and the ham, and place over the meat, with the shallots very finely chopped.

Now roll it up, and secure it with skewers or string. It is a good idea to tie it in a piece of the old-fashioned mutton cloth so successfully used by our grandmothers.

Put the hambone or bacon rinds at the bottom of a large saucepan with any tongue trimmings, salt, pepper, bouquet garni and chopped celery.

Put in the breast, cover with water or stock and simmer for about 3 hours, according to size of the breast.

When tender, remove and serve hot with thick brown gravy or tomato sauce. Any vegetables in season accompany this dish.

If you want to eat it cold, take off the cloth, if used, put the breast into a straight-sided vessel which fits it as well as can be, such as a cake tin. Half an ounce of gelatine dissolved in ¼ pint warm stock or water should be poured over at this stage. Put a plate on top, well-weighted, to firm the meat, and chill thoroughly.

Mutton or Lamb Cutlets à la Nelson

For 4 servings:

8 mutton cutlets	2 oz butter
1 egg and breadcrumbs	3 oz cooked macaroni or
4 oz lean ham	small tin spaghetti
	White sauce

Mince the ham finely and spread in a plate for dipping. Trim the cutlets into neat shapes. Dip each into beaten egg, then in the minced ham, then once more in the egg, and finally coat with breadcrumbs.

Melt the butter and when it is very hot put in the cutlets carefully. Fry briskly on each side, and remove to a hot dish.

The macaroni or spaghetti should be ready and hot at this stage. Put this in the middle of your dish, surrounded by the cutlets, and pour white sauce carefully into the centre. Brown gravy should be served separately, with vegetables in season.

Savoury Lamb Chops

Allow 2 lamb chops per person
8 oz diced cooked potatoes
8 oz diced cooked boiled bacon or ham
Small tin of baked beans

For savoury sauce:
2 onions
1 green pepper – parboiled and de-seeded
2 tomatoes
2 oz sliced mushrooms
$\frac{1}{2}$ tsp. mace
Clove of garlic, if liked
$\frac{1}{4}$ pint of stock or water
1 tsp. flour

Lightly fry chops on each side. Heat the diced potatoes and bacon. Arrange chops, potatoes and bacon in a fireproof dish and keep warm.

In an ounce of butter, gently fry all the sauce's ingredients. When thoroughly coated and beginning to colour, add thickening and stock, and cook covered for 20 minutes.

Pour over the chops, and garnish with chopped parsley.

Moussaka

This is a deliciously tasty dish, the aubergines giving it a distinctive tang, but quite substantial. Green vegetables or peas or beans will be all that is needed to serve with it.

1 lb lean minced mutton	½ lb tomatoes
(fresh or cooked)	3 tabs. olive oil
1 large onion	1 clove garlic
3 large aubergines	3 tabs. stock
	Seasoning

Cheese sauce:

2 tabs. butter	⅓ pint milk
2 tabs. flour	3 oz grated cheese

Put half the oil into one pan, heat it and brown the minced meat and chopped onion. Put the rest in another pan and lightly fry the peeled and finely sliced aubergine in it. Cook ingredients of both pans for about 10 minutes. Put meat into a fireproof shallow dish. Moisten with the stock and season with salt and cayenne pepper. Arrange cooked aubergine on top.

Skin and slice the tomatoes, and cook for a few minutes in the oil in which the aubergines were cooked. Put the well-crushed clove of garlic in with them. Put the tomatoes on top of the aubergines.

Now make the cheese sauce by melting the butter, stirring in the flour and allowing it to cook for a minute or two. Add the milk, bring to the boil, add the grated cheese and stir. Season to taste, and pour over the prepared dish. A further scattering of grated cheese can top all, if desired.

Bake in a moderate oven for about 30 minutes. It won't spoil if it is kept waiting a little while, and it is a dish which is good-natured enough to be made in advance and heated when needed.

If you prefer a green salad to hot green vegetables, with this dish, it is equally good.

One of the most spectacular lamb dishes is *Roast Crown of Lamb*. Better still, it is quite simple to cook, and also inexpensive, but you must have the co-operation of your butcher.

You are really cooking cutlets, of course, so allow 2, or possibly 3, for each person. The crown consists of two best-end necks of lamb, each having 6 or 7 cutlets. Let the butcher know a day or two in advance and he will make the crown by tying the two pieces of neck together, and cutting part-way between each cutlet for easy carving at the table.

Brush the joint with melted butter, and choose the type of stuffing from among these suggestions.

(1) *Celery and Tomato*

> ¼ lb fresh white breadcrumbs
> 3 tabs. par-boiled chopped celery
> 3 skinned and chopped tomatoes
> Salt, pepper
> 1 oz butter

Melt the butter. Stir in the celery, tomatoes and seasoning. Add the breadcrumbs and mix to a firm paste.

(2) *Walnut and Apricot*

> 2 oz dried apricots (previously soaked for 24 hours)
> 1 oz chopped walnuts
> ¼ lb fresh white breadcrumbs
> Juice of a lemon
> 1 oz butter

Melt the butter. Chop up the apricots very finely. Add them, the walnuts, lemon juice and breadcrumbs. Mix to a firm paste.

(3) *Sweet corn and Shallot*

> Small tin of sweet corn
> 2 finely chopped shallots
> ¼ lb fresh white breadcrumbs
> Salt and pepper
> 1 oz butter

Melt the butter. Drain the sweet corn.

Add sweet corn, chopped shallots, seasoning and breadcrumbs to form a firm paste.

In earlier days the cavity was sometimes filled with potato chips when brought to the table. Mashed potato is another simple and sensible filling, and I saw recently a hot cooked cauliflower fitted neatly into the basket formed by the bones. Personally, I prefer something simple like this, which is cooked separately and inserted before dishing up, but of course a savoury stuffing does add flavour to the crown in cooking.

If you decide to stuff the crown and then cook it, you must allow about 2 hours in a moderate oven. Baste frequently, with melted butter in the roasting pan, and remember to protect the top bones with foil so that they are not burnt.

Cutlet frills replace the foil when you bring it to the table. Some people use glacé cherries or olives instead. Cooked prunes, alternating with cutlet frills, also look attractive.

Some of you may have come across *The Diary of a Farmer's Wife*. Anne Hughes, a young married woman whose husband farmed in Herefordshire, kept the diary in 1796 and 1797, and very good reading it is.

She was a lively young woman and a good cook. The original spelling makes uneasy reading to begin with, but one soon gets used to it. I am including this recipe of hers for stuffed leg of mutton because I think you will be amused by her desire to 'wipe the eye' of Mistress Ellis, who was rather a busybody, and may like to try this very sound recipe.

Stuffed Leg of Mutton

'I doe from the legge cutt out a thick slice verie carefull, then I doe fill itt wyth a mess made off a cutte up union, tyme and parsley, and two eggs cooked harde, thys bee all chopt upp together whyth sum fatte bacon, then I doe push alle intoe the mutten ande presse inn thee cutt oute piece, ande tye itte harde whyth twyne toe hold itt furm, wile itt doe cooke, when itte bee colde I doe take away thee twyne ande itte doe cutte oute furm.

Iff Mistress Ellis doe cum, I shall give her some butte shalle notte telle her what makes thee fine flavour, shee bein sure too quiss, butte I shalle notte saye, so shee will be madd.'

Mutton Olives

Cold mutton makes very good olives, but the forcemeat should be really tasty. Minced veal and ham, bound with beaten egg, and flavoured with suitable herbs, makes an excellent stuffing. I once had them stuffed with a filling of curried rice with minced bacon and it was very good. Be ingenious with scraps of liver, mushrooms, olives, tomatoes or aubergines to create a toothsome stuffing.

When you have done so, put a nice dollop on one end of your mutton slice, roll it up and secure it with string.

Put the rolls in a baking tin, or a shallow fireproof dish which can be brought to the table, pour good gravy round them, cover with foil or the casserole lid, and cook fairly slowly for three-quarters of an hour. Serve with mashed potato and red-currant jelly.

Shepherd's Pie

This is, of course, *Cottage Pie* (page 65) but made with mutton or lamb. You will find the recipe under that name. I like leeks or onions in white sauce served with shepherd's pie in winter-time. Fresh garden peas or young French beans are delicious in the summer.

Bordeaux Mutton

Here is another good way of dealing with cold mutton or lamb. Cut the meat into nice collops. Brown some onions or shallots in butter. Put in the collops and brown them quickly on both sides. A rasher or two of bacon can be treated in the same way.

Put all into a casserole. Season with salt, pepper and any suitable herbs. Add a generous glassful of white wine. Cover and simmer for three-quarters of an hour.

Potted meat has always been recognized as a useful and tasty dish. The following delightful recipe occurs in a small book of 'Old Kentish Recipes'. The manuscript has been kept for many years in a friend's family. He kindly lent me the book and I only wish I could include some of the hair-raising remedies, parti-cularly the one 'For the Biting of a Mad Dog'. The dog is also given a dose!

But I must not stray too far from the culinary path, so here is an eighteenth-century recipe:

'To Pott Venison or Beefe in Slices

Cutte your venison or beefe in Collops an Inch thick. Lard them with bacon, season them high with pepper salt and nutmig. Lay butter on the bottom of your pott, then Lay in a Lay of Collops, then Lay in some slices of the good fatt of an Ox being seasoned as ye Collops, then lay in more ofthe Collops, then more of the said fatt, thus do till ye potts be full.

Lay on some butter and 2 bay leaves on ye top, paper and cover it with course past, bake it tender, pour out the Gravy and fill it up with clarified butter. Lay a weight on it whilst it is hott that ye fatt and Collops may be congeale together.

If you would have it Redd add a little Salt peter.

Serve it with Mustard and Sugger.'

Oxford John

The recipe for this dish is given among the beef recipes, but it is equally good made with thin slices of raw lamb or mutton. Lean collops cut from the shoulder are very good and tender, but slices from the leg can also be recommended.

Noisettes of Lamb

Allow two small lamb chops per person.

> 8 best end of neck or loin lamb chops
> 2 oz mushrooms
> 4 large tomatoes
> 2 oz butter
> Seasoning

Bone and roll the chops, and tie each into a neat round parcel with string. Stand them in the grill pan with a dab of butter on each.

Now cut tomatoes in half and carefully scoop out the pulp. Melt about an ounce of the butter, and lightly fry the finely-chopped mushroom and tomato pulp together. Season to taste, and fill the tomato cups. Put a dab of butter on each and put beside the noisettes in the grill pan.

Cook for about 15 minutes under the grill, basting occasionally, or bake in a fairly hot oven for about 30 minutes.

Another way to cook noisettes of lamb:

Curried Noisettes of Lamb

8 boned and rolled lamb chops	4 oz mushrooms
	8 tomatoes
1 oz butter	1 dessertspoon mild curry

Cream the curry with the butter and spread on both sides of the chops which you have tied neatly with string. Put under a hot grill for a few minutes, to brown quickly on both sides, then remove to a greased dish for finishing in a moderate oven – a further 25–30 minutes.

Grease another fireproof dish ready for tomatoes and mushrooms. Wipe the tomatoes and cut a cross on the skin at the top. Take off mushroom stalks and put, with the tomatoes, black side up, into the second dish. Dot with butter and allow 15–20 minutes for cooking in the oven.

At the time of writing, chicken is about the cheapest meat available. It has many other advantages. It is a light but nutritious meat, it blends well with other ingredients, and is equally good hot or cold.

If you are lucky enough to have a fine upstanding bird which has spent a happy life scratching freely about the farmyard or nearby field, pecking at such delectable fodder as fresh chickweed, young dandelion leaves and good corn, then of course you cannot do better than roast it in the traditional way, probably on your new rotary spit, and bring it triumphantly to the table with its accompanying bread sauce, bacon rolls and general fragrant glory.

It is much more likely that your chicken will be shrouded in a polythene bag, and will be dropped on the draining board by the butcher boy with 'the sound of iron on stone' to await your ministrations the next day.

It is generally admitted that the broiler birds lack flavour, so experiment with herbs, spices, stuffings and garnishings. The first recipe is one which I use frequently. I have also used it with pheasant, and have no doubt that a small turkey would be very good treated in the same way.

It is as easy as falling off a log to cook. If your guests are a little late it won't spoil for waiting, and no matter how insipid your chicken, in the raw, it will emerge very appetizing.

Chicken Stanley

1 chicken	¼ lb butter
2–3 large onions	1 glass white wine
3 tabs. double cream	Salt and pepper

Slice onions into a deep casserole large enough to take the bird. Dot with butter.

Put a large piece of butter inside the chicken and brush outside with a little melted butter. Put the bird on top of the onions, cover, and cook in a moderate oven for about 1½–2 hours.

Turn the bird occasionally during cooking and baste well with the onion-flavoured butter. The glass of wine, salt and pepper, should be added after about 20 minutes cooking time.

Remove lid about 15 minutes before serving to allow the bird to brown. Strain the onion (a slotted spoon is useful for this) and put it into a little dish to be served separately. Reduce the cooking liquor to about ½ pint, add the cream, and pour this sauce over the chicken or serve separately. The addition of a small teaspoonful of curry powder to the sauce is liked by some people.

Chicken Timbales

½ lb minced cooked chicken
2 eggs
1 tab. chopped parsley

4 tabs. white breadcrumbs
6 tabs. milk
Pepper and salt

Warm the milk in a saucepan and add the beaten egg, soft breadcrumbs, parsley, the minced chicken and seasoning.

Butter small tins, moulds, or ramekins and press the mixture to about two-thirds of their depth.

Stand the little dishes in a bain-marie and bake in a gentle oven for about half an hour. They are deliciously light, either hot or cold, and will often tempt an invalid's jaded appetite.

Try spinach, sweet corn, or puréed tomatoes with them if served hot. A green salad is good if they are served cold.

Smothered Chicken

This somewhat gruesomely named dish is very simple to make, and deliciously bland.

1 boiled fowl
1 pint of white sauce

Simmer the fowl in a home-cooked *court-bouillon*, or a chicken cube will do nearly as well, for about 1½ hours.

Lift from liquor, joint neatly and arrange on a hot dish.

Make a good white sauce, which you may like to transform by adding chopped parsley or chopped mushroom. Coat the joints well and serve with the remainder of the sauce in a sauceboat.

Rice Salad

This is a most useful dish as it can be made in any season with the vegetables which are available. It adds something interesting and substantial to a cold-meat-and-green-salad meal, and is very attractive to the eye.

> 4 tab. Patna rice
> 1 medium tin sweet corn
> ½ cucumber
> 1 tab. chopped nuts
> 1 tab. washed sultanas

Chopped celery, spring onion, endive, chives, parsley, apple, etc. In fact, anything in season which will blend well. Finely grated carrot, finely chopped red peppers, radishes and olives all add colour as well as taste.

If you like garlic, rub the serving bowl well with a cut clove before piling in the rice salad.

Cook the rice for 12 minutes. Drain and add the drained sweet corn. This is the basis of your salad. Now add available ingredients and a drop or two of olive oil.

Blend well together, add salt and white pepper to taste, and turn into an attractive bowl, preferably a wooden one.

Sweets

Most people these days prefer the sweet or pudding course to be light and simple. Fresh fruit in season cannot be beaten, but now and again a cook likes to provide something a little more adventurous.

As rationing slowly died away after the last war, there was a natural resurgence of interest in those rich sweets of which we had been starved so long. It was the heyday of elaborate trifles and mousses sicklied o'er with angelica and glacé cherries. One was not even spared those silver balls which are calculated to crack every stopping in the molars. Monstrous shapes, like tea-cosies, abounded, with cream piped down every crack in sight.

But the fever has largely passed, thank goodness, and it is interesting to see the revival of the light, rather plain puddings, of the Victorians (when they are made at all) in today's kitchens. Bread and Butter Pudding, Queen of Puddings, and certain steamed puddings are making a welcome return, particularly in the colder months and where there are children to be fed.

But, on the whole, the recipes I give for sweets will be light. The dangers of being overweight make many of us wary of too-rich food, and a bowl of fresh fruit supplies most of us with an adequate sweet course. You will find most of our native fruit recipes, naturally, in the Summer and Autumn sections, but here are some sweets and puddings which can be made in the rather colder days of Spring.

Fresh-sliced Oranges

4 large Jaffa oranges
3 oz caster sugar
Dessertspoonful of cointreau, grand marnier,
aurum or any orange liqueur

When peeling oranges, *warm* them first. The major part of the pith will come away easily then with the peel.

Slice them across as finely as possible and remove any pips. Put the orange circles in the dish in which they will be served, and strew with a little caster sugar and a drop or two of the liqueur.

Continue in layers until all the ingredients are used up. Cover with a plate or polythene cover so that all can become nicely blended, and let it stand for 2 or 3 hours.

Some people like to chill this dish in the refrigerator before serving. Personally, I think the flavour is better when citrus fruits are not served too cold, particularly if a liqueur has been added, but it is a lovely sweet either way.

Rhubarb Fluff

There is usually plenty of forced rhubarb about in the early months of the year. Plain stewed is rather dreary, but this simple recipe makes the most of its tart freshness.

2 lb forced rhubarb
5–6 oz caster sugar (preferably vanilla-flavoured)
⅛ pint double cream

Chop the rhubarb into short pieces and simmer until soft with the sugar and 3 tabs. of water. Whisk to a purée or put into the electric blender.

Whip the cream, not too stiffly, fold into the rhubarb, and serve very cold.

Vanilla sugar is best for this recipe, and in fact for most sweet recipes. Keep a large screw-top jar filled with caster sugar (mine is an outsize Maxwell House coffee jar). Tucked into the sugar should be one or two vanilla pods which you can buy, in a long glass tube, from any reputable grocer. These pods flavour the sugar beautifully, and will not need to be replaced – although the sugar will, of course, as you use it – for a year or more.

Queen of Puddings

½ pint milk   2 oz caster sugar
1 oz butter   ½ tsp. grated lemon rind
2 eggs   1 tab. jam
2½ oz white breadcrumbs

Heat the milk and butter together with half the sugar. Now beat in the breadcrumbs and let the mixture stand for 10 minutes.

Separate the yolks and whites of the eggs. Beat the yolks and add them to the mixture. Now add the grated lemon rind.

Put the mixture into a shallow greased fireproof dish, and bake in a moderate oven for about 25 minutes until it is firm. When set, spread the jam over the surface. Stiffly whisk the whites, folding in the rest of the sugar at the end, and pile on top of the pudding. Return it to the oven for about 5–10 minutes to allow the meringue to brown.

Better, by far, eaten hot, but it can be served cold if preferred.

Plain Boiled Custard

To make one pint of custard you will need:

¾ pint milk
⅛ pint thin cream
2 whole eggs
2 egg yolks
2 tabs. sugar

Put 2 egg yolks with the contents of 2 whole eggs together in a basin and mix to a smooth, but not frothy, consistency.

Arrange a basin over a pan of boiling water, or use a double-boiler pan for your ingredients. Rinse the basin or top part of the boiler with cold water to prevent sticking later. Put in the ¾ pint of milk.

Add the thin cream to the eggs in the basin and stir together. When the milk is boiling, pour it over the egg mixture, add the sugar, and then return all to the top part of the boiler. Stir until it thickens, making sure that the water boils steadily the while.

When it is thick enough to coat a spoon, remove from heat, and turn it at once into the dish into which it will be served to prevent further cooking.

A custard made this way is extremely light, and can be flavoured by infusing finely cut lemon rind or a bay leaf in the milk as it warms. Some people prefer to add a few drops of almond or vanilla essence, at this stage, instead.

If vanilla-flavoured sugar is used this gives quite enough flavouring to the dish, of course.

Caramel Custard

This is always popular, and very simple to make. It is equally good hot or cold. Remember that these firmer custards need a larger proportion of eggs to the milk than boiled or baked custards which will not need to be turned out.

For 4 generous helpings:

> ¾ pint milk
> 4 eggs
> 1 oz caster sugar, vanilla-flavoured, if available
>
> *For the caramel*
> 3 oz loaf or granulated sugar
> 4 tabs. water

Prepare the caramel by stirring sugar and water until it boils. Then allow it to simmer on its own until it is golden brown.

Grease a plain fireproof dish – a soufflé dish is ideal – pour in the caramel and allow to cool.

Now blend together the eggs and sugar. Warm the milk and pour it on to the eggs. Pour through a strainer into the caramel-prepared dish.

Stand the dish in a bain-marie, or baking tin with water halfway up the sides, and bake in a slow oven for about three quarters of an hour or until custard is set.

It will need care in turning out. The caramel will have melted, naturally, and will form the pudding's delicious sauce.

You can put the mixture into individual dishes if so desired. They will take only about half the time to cook in the oven.

When one has used the whites of eggs only or, alternatively, the yolks only, in a certain recipe, it is always a problem to know how to finish up the remaining component parts. One can't always be making meringues or serving scrambled eggs!

Here is an obliging pair of complementary recipes supplied by a friend. They are very economical, light and refreshing, and look well served together – one snowy white and the other yellow.

New Zealand Sweet

2 cups water
1½ cups caster sugar
Rind of 1 lemon

2 tabs. cornflour
Juice of 2 lemons
Whites of 2 eggs

Bring all ingredients, except egg whites, to the boil together to thicken. Remove lemon rind, and allow mixture to cool. When nearly cold fold in the stiffly-beaten whites of egg. Put in a mould, chill, and serve with cream.

To use the yolks:

2 cups water
1 cup caster sugar
2 tabs. cornflour

2 egg yolks
1 oz butter
Grated rind and juice of 1 lemon

Make a paste with the cornflour and a little of the water. Put the rest of the ingredients, with the exception of the egg yolks, into a saucepan to heat. Pour half into the cornflour paste, then return all to the saucepan stirring over a gentle heat.

Beat egg yolks well, and add to mixture. Stir until the mixture thickens but does not boil. Pour into a mould and serve when very cold.

Pavlova

This makes an elegant sweet. I like to see it completely white, adding point to its name, but some people prefer to use coloured fruit or ice-cream, or a mixture of both, as the filling.

For a case (or cases) for 4–6 people you will need:

4 egg whites
8 oz caster sugar
1 tsp. cornflour

A few drops of wine vinegar and vanilla essence

Beat egg whites stiffly and fold in the sugar gradually, adding the cornflour with the last spoonful of sugar.

Fold in the vinegar and vanilla essence.

Spread the mixture on a piece of paper which has been brushed with oil or melted butter. Shape it to form a flan or shell, and put it into a barely warm oven to dry. It will take several hours to become really firm. Use a warmed knife to lift the fragile case – or cases – from the paper.

When cold, fill it with vanilla ice cream and sliced white tinned peaches or pears. If you prefer to see your Pavlova with more colour, then well-drained tinned fruit, or better still, such bright fruit as fresh strawberries, raspberries or peeled grapes will all look very attractive.

This dish should be eaten at one sitting. It will not keep firm once the shell has been filled.

Chestnut Cream

1 15-oz tin chestnut purée *naturel*
1½ tab. vanilla sugar
½ oz gelatine
4 tabs. milk
2 tabs. cream, and enough cream for masking

Dissolve the gelatine in tepid milk in a saucepan. Add the purée and sugar and blend all together thoroughly. Remove from heat, beat in the cream and turn into a wetted mould.

Chill well, turn out carefully and mask with whipped cream.

Cakes

Cakes seem to be sadly unfashionable just now which is a great pity for the keen cook. All cooking is an art, but with cake-making particularly the scientific approach is also important.

It does not matter when making a beef dish *en casserole*, say, if you put in 2 or 4 carrots. If you are stewing apples, no one will cavil if you put in an extra spoonful of sugar by mistake.

But cake-making is an exact science, and omitting half a teaspoonful of baking powder can turn a triumph into a disaster. It is this challenge which true cooks enjoy in making cakes, and which makes their successes so rewarding.

I shall not touch on yeast cookery nor give recipes for those rich and delectable confections known in the trade as *gateaux*. But those of us who live in the country, several miles from shops, are particularly vulnerable to chance visitors, and need to have something ready in the cake-tin to offer them.

Here are three staunch favourites which have seen me through many a surprise visitation. All three keep well in air-tight tins. The Dundee cake and shortbread will keep literally for weeks, and the Victoria sandwich for at least a week. The latter can be whipped up with the minimum of fuss, if you have an hour or so's notice, and filled with home-made jam, lemon curd or fresh cream is welcomed by anyone from eight months old to eighty.

Dundee Cake

10 oz plain flour	5 eggs
8 oz sugar	$\frac{1}{4}$ tsp. bicarbonate of soda
8 oz butter	3 oz blanched almonds

2 oz candied peel
2 oz glacé cherries
1 tab. milk

Grated rind of 1 orange
1 lb mixed sultanas and currants

Cream sugar and butter. Add beaten eggs and a little sifted flour very gradually, blending well until mixture is smooth.

Stir in the rest of the flour with the washed and dried fruit, the chopped cherries, half the almonds, chopped, the candied peel and grated orange rind.

Dissolve the bicarbonate of soda in the milk, and add to the mixture, stirring well.

Grease and line an 8-inch cake-tin, and put in the cake mixture. Spread the rest of the almonds, unchopped, on top, and bake in a very slow oven for about 3 hours, or until a probing skewer comes out clean.

Shortbread

$\frac{1}{2}$ lb plain flour
$\frac{1}{4}$ lb butter
3 oz caster sugar

Cream butter and sugar. Add flour and mix lightly until the mixture has the look of breadcrumbs.

Press the mixture into a greased sandwich tin to a depth of about $\frac{1}{2}$ inch. Bake in a slow oven for about 40 minutes. Cut into pieces whilst still warm.

Victoria Sandwich

4 oz butter, Trex or Spry
4 oz caster sugar
4 oz plain flour

1 tsp. baking powder
2 eggs
1 tab. warm water

Cream butter and sugar until fluffy. Beat eggs and add gradually. Add warm water and beat well.

Add sifted flour and baking powder, and stir thoroughly until the mixture will spread easily.

Put into two well-greased and floured sandwich tins. (Don't forget to put a small piece of greaseproof paper at the bottom to ease turning out.)

Bake in a moderate oven for about 20 minutes.

Cinnamon Sponge

4 oz butter
4 oz caster sugar
2 eggs
5 oz flour

Tsp. baking powder
2 tabs. warm water
Dessertspn. cinnamon
Dessertspn. golden syrup

Cream butter and sugar. Beat the eggs and add gradually.

Sift in the flour, baking powder and cinnamon. Melt golden syrup in the water, and beat into the mixture. If the mixture seems too dry, a little milk may be added to bring it to a thickish batter consistency.

Beat well, then pour it into two greased and floured sandwich tins. Bake for about 20 minutes in a moderate oven.

Useful note: To ease the turning-out problem with sponge sandwiches, put a strip of greaseproof paper, about 2 in. by 1 in. will be about right, into the base of the tin after greasing and flouring. Or spread a wet tea-cloth over the inverted tins as they cool.

Chocolate Brownies

There is a nice crunchiness about these unusual little cakes. Very popular – particularly with children.

2 oz walnuts
3 oz butter
4 oz flour
2 oz caster sugar

2 oz plain chocolate
1 egg
¼ tsp. baking powder
¼ tsp. salt
Milk to mix

Chop the walnuts and melt the chocolate in a basin over hot water.

Cream together butter and sugar, and add well-beaten egg. Sift in flour, baking powder and salt, and mix well.

Now add nuts, melted chocolate and a very little milk, just enough to bring it to a soft consistency.

Spread mixture into a greased baking tin and dredge a little sugar on top. Bake in a moderate oven for 30 minutes.

Cut into neat squares or fingers whilst still warm.

Flapjacks

6 oz butter
8 oz caster sugar
5 oz porridge oats
3 oz desiccated coconut
4 oz plain chocolate for covering, if liked

Cream sugar and butter, and mix in the oats and coconut. Stir well together and press into a large shallow tin – 12 in. by 6 in. is ideal – to a depth of about ½ inch.

Cook in a moderate oven for about 25 minutes, or until golden brown.

To make this doubly delicious and fattening, melt 4 oz plain chocolate and spread over the cooked flapjack. Make curly squiggles with a fork, and when cold cut into neat fingers.

Lemon Curd

I always think of this, with the exception of marmalade, as the first preserve of the year, and probably the most popular. It is, without doubt, the one which proves the superiority of the home-made over the bought product.

3 oz butter
3 large eggs
6 oz caster sugar
Rind and juice of 2 lemons

Put butter, sugar, lemon juice and very finely grated rind into a basin, and stand this over a pan of boiling water. Blend all together, and when butter has melted, add the eggs, well-whisked, to the other ingredients.

Stir until mixture thickens, which will take about 20 minutes. Pour into warmed jars and cover when cold.

Summer

Summer, for the cook, means delicious young vegetables, broad beans, peas, baby carrots, pearly spring onions, and salad stuffs fresh from the garden. It also brings the choicest of the soft fruits, the strawberries and raspberries, the gooseberries and currants, red, white and black.

Salmon and fresh trout are at their best, and English lamb comes into its own. Weather permitting, it is picnic time, and pâté and mousse, both sweet and savoury, can be added to the sandwiches in the picnic basket.

Cherries are grown extensively in these parts, and one of the highlights of the summer is the trip across the Downs to a fruit farm where the fruit stands, basket upon basket, in a huge thatched barn. There are dozens of varieties, with splendid names such as Napoleon and White Hearts, all equally tempting. And as well as cherries there are raspberries, red currants and ripe strawberries as fat as stuffed pincushions.

It is this last fruit which takes me back over the years to a childhood in Kent. There, in the summer, the strawberry fields smelt ambrosial. When the crop was picked and the best of it had rumbled up to Covent Garden, the fruit grower used to let anyone so minded pick those that were left.

Mostly they were small, but exactly right for jam. Always there seemed to be some fine specimens left among rustling straw, and these we ate.

The jam which was made was particularly relished because we had picked the fruit ourselves, and the smell of strawberry jam cooking always reminds me of those sunny days nearly half a century ago.

You will find a recipe in this section on pages 134–5.

Soups

Summer Soup

This light clear soup can be embellished with any summer vegetable with which your garden happens to be blessed. French beans, peas, asparagus and young carrots lend themselves beautifully.

> ½ pint mixed vegetables, as above
> 2 pints clear stock
> Seasoning

Slice, dice or cut into small attractive shapes, the available vegetables. Cook in salted water until soft, then drain.

Bring stock to the boil, add vegetables and seasoning, and serve very hot.

Fresh Green Pea Soup

Spare some of the peas from those rows in the garden for this exquisitely fragrant summer soup.

1 pint peas and their shells	Tsp. sugar – sprig of mint
A handful of spinach	1½ pints white stock
1 oz butter	½ pint milk

Simmer peas, their shells and spinach with a sprig of mint and the sugar in the stock until all are tender. Strain through sieve, but keep a few peas back for garnishing.

Return to saucepan, add milk and butter, and reheat. Garnish with peas before serving with croûtons.

Or try this version:

1½ pints shelled peas
1 substantial lettuce heart
3 oz butter

2 pints water
2 tsp. sugar
Salt

Wash and shred lettuce. Melt butter in saucepan and put in lettuce, shelled peas, salt and sugar. Cook very slowly for 10–12 minutes, shaking now and again so that all is thoroughly mixed with the melted butter. Now add the water, and cook until peas are tender. Sieve, return to pan, season, and reheat.

Cherry Soup

This recipe is of Basque origin, but for those lucky enough to have salvaged cherries from the attentive birds here is an unusual soup to make with them.

4 cupfuls stoned cherries
2 pints cold water
Half cup caster sugar

Tab. arrowroot
Juice of half a lemon
Tab. cherry brandy

Simmer the cherries in the water with sugar until tender. Pass it through a sieve and return it to the pan. Blend the arrowroot with a little cold water, add to the pan and cook for 8–10 minutes. Allow it to cool, add lemon juice and cherry brandy. Chill before serving.

Asparagus Cream Soup

This is perhaps the queen of white soups.

About 12 asparagus tips or   2 oz butter
half a bundle, if bought   1 oz flour
2 pints white stock – pre-   2 tabs. cream
ferably chicken   Salt and pepper

Make a thin white sauce with butter, flour and stock. Carefully clean, scrape and cut asparagus into short lengths. Put a few of the extreme tips to cook separately in a little salted water; they will take only a few minutes to become tender.

Put cut lengths into stock and simmer for 30 minutes. Draw the pan from the heat before adding cream and the drained tips. Serve very hot, but do not allow to boil again.

Cold Cucumber Soup

2 cucumbers   Salt and white pepper to
1 onion   taste
1 oz butter   1 pint milk
1 oz cornflour   1 pint white stock
2 oz grated cheese   2 tabs. cream

Sauté onion in butter, thicken with the cornflour, stirring gently. Add chopped and peeled cucumbers, and mixed milk and stock. Season to taste, and simmer until cucumber is soft. Add grated cheese and cook for a further 5 minutes. Put through mill or sieve, stir in cream, and when cool store in refrigerator. Two or three finely cut cucumber rings make a pleasing garnish to this cold soup when served.

Here is an old Kentish recipe supplied by a friend in whose family the book has been for generations. At a guess, I should say that this is an early nineteenth-century recipe.

'A Lettice Soup. Miss Lee – very good

Take a quantity of Lettice leaves and Fry them in butter. They must be cut in pieces and the stalks taken out. Let them be brown, but not burnt, when done put in a quart or as much boiling water as you chuse, a Pint or more of young green pease, whole Pepper and salt and a Bundle of sweet herbs, let all this stew together an hour or more till the pease are quite tender, then thicken it with a piece of Butter rolled in flour, stir it well, and it is done.'

This is a useful summer soup recipe, especially when the lettuces in the garden are beginning to 'bolt' because the family cannot keep pace with them.

Hors d'oeuvre

Tomato and Egg

This individual hors d'oeuvre makes a pretty dish and is extremely simple to prepare.

 1 large tomato and 1 hard-boiled egg for each person
 A little lettuce or cress for the bed
 Thick mayonnaise

Stand tomato firmly on its stalk end and, with a sharp knife, slice from the top almost to the base about 6 to 8 times. The tomato should then fan open rather like the pages of a book.

Into each gap slide a slice of hard-boiled egg. Top with a spoonful of mayonnaise and a pinch of paprika or chopped parsley. Serve on the greenery.

Egg Mayonnaise

Allow one hard-boiled egg for each person. Put a dessertspoonful of good mayonnaise in the centre of each dish. Cut each egg lengthwise and put side down upon the little golden pool. Sprinkle with chopped parsley. Surround with a little greenery.

This is simple, satisfying and always popular.

Pineapple and Cheese Salad

This is a pretty dish and very refreshing.

Pineapple rings, allow one, or two at the most, per person
3 oz cream cheese, not too salt
Mayonnaise to bind mixture

Blend cream cheese with sufficient mayonnaise to be malleable enough to form the mixture into small balls.

Arrange drained pineapple rings on a bed of lettuce leaves and put a cream cheese ball on each. Decorate with a slice of olive or a sprinkling of paprika, if so desired.

Mint Grapefruit Cocktail

Allow one grapefruit per person
1 tsp. Crème de Menthe
1 tsp. caster sugar

Cut the grapefruit in half and remove segments. Keep any juice that spills during this operation.

Put segments and juice into individual glasses and blend in a teaspoonful of sugar and Crème de Menthe.

Chill thoroughly. Serve garnished with small sprig of mint. This is very pretty and refreshing on a hot day.

Melon with Prawns

8 oz fresh or frozen prawns
1 small melon
4 tabs. double cream
1 tab. of each of the following finely chopped: Green or red peppers and tarragon
4 tabs. mayonnaise and a dash of Tabasco, salt and pepper, and 1 tab. tomato ketchup.

Mix together mayonnaise, tomato ketchup, chopped peppers, tarragon and cream. Season to taste, adding Tabasco with discretion.

Peel melon, take out seeds and dice the flesh. Mix with sauce and the prawns. Serve the mixture, thoroughly chilled, in individual dishes garnished with a sprig of water cress.

Swiss Eggs

Delicious but rather rich. It makes a very good prelude to a cold main course.

1 egg per person
4 tabs. cream
4 oz grated cheese
Pepper and salt

Butter a shallow fireproof dish, and spread thickly with most of the grated cheese. Put a spoonful of cream ready for each egg, on top of the cheese, and make a dent to hold each egg. Break an egg into each cavity and use up the cream by filling in the cracks. Season with pepper and salt and cover with more grated cheese.

Cook for 15 minutes in a fairly hot oven (Mark 5 gas or 380° electricity). Serve hot.

Minced cooked ham can be substituted for the bottom layer, but takes a little longer to cook.

Cheese and Salmon Soufflé

1 oz butter
1 oz flour
2 oz grated cheese
3 eggs

4 oz flaked cooked salmon or
1 small tin of salmon
¼ pint milk
Salt and pepper

Melt the butter, stir in the flour, and work in the milk. Bring to boiling point, stirring until thick. Season the sauce.

Pour half over the salmon and mix well. Spread this mixture into a shallow fireproof dish. Into the remaining half of the sauce blend the grated cheese and the yolks of the 3 eggs, one at a time. Beat well.

Whisk 3 whites stiffly and fold into this mixture. Spread over the salmon and bake in a hot oven for about 15-20 minutes. Serve immediately.

Ratatouille

This is a useful dish because it is equally good hot or cold, so make enough to use the next day.

2 Spanish onions
2 green or red peppers
2 aubergines
2 baby marrows (courgettes)

1 tab. chopped parsley
Pinch of marjoram and basil
Clove of garlic, chopped finely
Olive oil – about 4 or 5 tabs.

Slice onion finely and cook in the oil. Remove seeds and stalks from peppers. Chop with baby marrows and aubergines and add to onion. Season with salt and pepper. Cover pan and cook slowly for about 30 minutes. Add herbs and garlic. Cook a further 10 minutes. Drain off surplus oil. Serve very hot.

Egg and Spinach

Probably one of the lightest and most nourishing dishes possible. Particularly so if the spinach is fresh from the garden and the eggs from hens that run about freely.

Cook spinach. Poach an egg for each person and serve individually on a bed of spinach. Or put the spinach in a large dish, place the eggs on it, cover thickly with grated cheese and put under a hot grill for a moment or two. Or, if preferred, pour over Mornay sauce instead of the raw grated cheese.

Main Dishes

We are fortunate here for our village is not far from those two great trout rivers, the Kennet and the Lambourn. Generous neighbours, who fish these waters, often arrive with a fresh-caught trout - a most welcome present.

If you are lucky enough to have a whopper to cook then I think the best way to tackle it is to wrap it securely in well-buttered foil and bake it in a moderate oven for up to an hour. Serve on a hot dish with the juices, and that is that.

Grilling or frying a large fish is not satisfactory because the heat does not penetrate to the middle until the outside is scorched. But for smaller fish, try these recipes.

Grilled Trout

This is considered the best way, by far, of cooking trout.

Clean the fish. Dot with butter (clarified is best) and grill on both sides until done - usually about 10 minutes for a smallish trout.

Fried Trout

2 or 3 trout
1 egg
Breadcrumbs

Clarified butter for frying
1 lemon

Clean and fillet the fish. Sprinkle with salt and then dry it.

Beat up the egg, dip in the fillets and sprinkle with dried breadcrumbs. Heat the butter until a blue smoke arises. Put in the fillets, which will fry very quickly.

Drain and serve with lemon wedges.

These fillets can be used cold in aspic jelly, served with green salad.

Trout in White Wine

Clean the fish and put in a shallow casserole. Cover with white wine in which chopped onion, salt, pepper and two or three cloves have steeped. Cook, covered, in a gentle oven for about half an hour.

Trout with Almonds

A trout per person	3 oz butter
3 tabs. seasoned flour	3 oz blanched split almonds

Clean fish, wipe dry. Coat each fish with seasoned flour and fry in very hot melted butter on each side until golden brown. Keep hot.

Lower heat under the butter. Add the almonds and fry gently until browned slightly.

Pour hot butter and almonds over the trout and serve very hot, with lemon wedges.

Trout in Oatmeal (Scotch recipe)

A trout per person	Butter for frying
1 oz small-sized oatmeal	Lemon wedges

Treat the trout as in the recipe above, but bone the trout first as one would a herring, and flatten it. Coat with the oatmeal, and fry in very hot butter until golden brown. Serve very hot with the lemon.

It is interesting to note that Eliza Acton whose classic cookery book was published in 1845 only gives one recipe for trout, and that is for 'Stewed Trout'. She does, however, add the following note:

'Trout may be stewed in equal parts of strong veal gravy, and of red or white wine, without having been previously browned; the sauce should then be thickened, and agreeably flavoured with lemon juice, and the usual store-sauces, before it is poured over the fish. They are also good when wrapped in buttered paper, and baked or broiled; if very small, the better mode of cooking is to fry them whole. They should never be plain boiled, as, though naturally a delicious fish, they are then very insipid.'

Eliza Acton's next recipes are for Pike. One is 'To Bake Pike (A Common Receipt)' and the next 'To Bake Pike (Superior Receipt)', so naturally I shall supply you with the latter.

Pike is rather neglected these days, and a great many people actively dislike its rather muddy flavour. Parson Woodforde frequently had 'a fine Pyke with a pudding in its belly' for one of his many courses. On May 18 1778 he writes:

'And we had the largest Pike we caught for dinner and it weighed 7 pounds. Mr Pounsett and Jenny said they never eat so fine a Fish in all their lives – it was prodigious nice indeed.'

Three days later, whilst fishing in the nearby Lenswade River, the good parson caught a pike 'which weighed 8 Pound and a half and it had in his Belly another Pike, of above a Pound. We caught also there the finest Trout I ever saw which weighed 3 Pound and two ounces.'

Here is Eliza Acton's Superior Receipt for those of you who enjoy pike.

'Scale and wash the fish, take out the gills, then open it just sufficiently to allow the inside to be emptied and *perfectly cleansed*, but not more than is necessary for that purpose. Wipe it dry . . . and fill the body with oyster-forcemeat, or with veal forcemeat; sew it up very securely, and curl it round, and fasten the tail into the mouth with a thin skewer, then dip it in the beaten yolks of two or more eggs, seasoned with nearly half a teaspoonful of salt, and a little pepper, or cayenne; cover it equally with the finest breadcrumbs, dip it a second time into the egg and crumbs, then pour some clarified butter gently over it, and send it to a well-heated oven for an hour and a quarter or more, should it be *very* large, but for less time if it be only of moderate size.'

Plaice is available all the year round, but is reckoned to be at its best from May until December. It is a fish which adapts itself to many forms of cooking, and although it is usually filleted and fried, it is equally good, particularly for invalids, when the fillets are rolled and cooked in milk.

Here are a few plaice recipes which are rather unusual. Lemon sole, if preferred can be substituted for plaice in these recipes.

Plaice with Bananas

> 4 fillets of plaice
> 2 bananas
> 2 oz butter
> 2 oz blanched almonds
> Juice of 1 lemon

Grease a shallow fireproof dish. Put the fillets in this, dotted with a little butter, and sprinkled with half the lemon juice. Cover and cook in moderate oven for 15 minutes.

Melt the rest of the butter in a frying-pan. Fry banana slices gently for about 3 minutes.

Put the fillets in a warm serving dish, and arrange fried banana over them.

Add remainder of lemon juice to the fat in the pan, and increase the heat. Brown the almonds in the butter and lemon juice, pour over the fillets and serve at once.

Plaice with Tomato and Caper Sauce

4 fillets of plaice	1 oz butter
1 small onion	1 dessertsp. capers
4 oz peeled tomatoes or	Salt and pepper
1 small tin tomatoes	

Arrange the fillets in a greased shallow casserole. Blend together finely chopped onion and the tomatoes. Season well and pour over the plaice. Dot with butter.

Cover and bake in a moderate oven for about 30 minutes.

Pour off the tomato and onion sauce, and sieve it. Stir in the capers and return to the casserole to heat again.

This is good with hot boiled rice or well-mashed potato.

Plaice Florentine

4 rolled fillets of plaice	1 lb spinach
1 oz butter	4 tabs. single cream
1 oz grated cheese (Parmesan	Salt and pepper
is best)	1 tsp. basil, if liked
1 tab. soft breadcrumbs	

Cook and sieve the spinach, and blend with the cream to a smooth consistency.

Season with salt, pepper and basil. Put the mixture at the bottom of a shallow greased casserole, and dot with a little of the butter.

Arrange rolled fillets on top. Sprinkle with the grated cheese and breadcrumbs. Dot with the rest of the butter.

Bake in a fairly hot oven for 20 minutes.

This is a tasty and nutritious way of serving plaice. Again lemon soles can be treated this way, or halibut or turbot collops.

Plaice Fritters

1½ lb filleted plaice	Small cupful tepid water
4 oz flour	2 egg whites
1 tab. olive oil	Salt
	Oil or fat for frying

Cut the plaice into small pieces, wiped and dried. Put the flour into a bowl, stir in olive oil, salt and tepid water. Beat to a smooth batter.

Before frying begins, add stiffly beaten egg whites. Immerse the fish pieces, then drop them into smoking fat. They will only take a few minutes to cook. Drain well before serving very hot, and garnished with parsley

Fish Soufflé

This is a deliciously light dish, more suited to hot weather than kedgeree, that other reliable way of using cooked flaked fish.

You will need for 4 people:

2 oz butter	6–8 oz cooked flaked fish
1 oz flour	3 eggs
¾ pint milk	Seasoning
	½ pint caper sauce

Make a white sauce with butter, flour and milk. Add pepper and salt, and a little finely grated onion if liked. Then add the fish. Remove from heat and stir in three well-beaten egg-yolks. Now beat the whites until stiff and fold gradually into the mixture. Put into greased soufflé dish, and stand this in a bain-marie, or baking tin containing water coming halfway up the sides of the dish.

Bake in a fairly hot oven for 15–20 minutes. Serve with caper sauce.

Whiting in White Wine

This useful fish is available all the year round, but its flavour is so delicate that it can easily be found insipid. It is cheap, nourishing, and easily digested. I have yet to meet the cat that refused whiting, and if cats like something, then it is usually very good indeed. This recipe gives the whiting an added fillip.

1 medium-sized boned whiting per person	1 oz butter
	Juice of 1 lemon
4 tabs. dry white wine	1 tab. chopped parsley
1 tab. French mustard	½ onion

Grease a shallow fireproof dish and place the whiting in it. Season, and sprinkle the onion, finely chopped, upon it.

Melt the butter in a saucepan, then add wine, mustard, lemon juice and parsley. When blended, pour this sauce over the fish, cover casserole, and bake in a moderate oven for 30–40 minutes.

The first fresh salmon comes into season in February, and the season continues until September. Consequently, 'The King of Fishes' is at its best throughout the summer months when it is often served cold, and its delicate flavour and appearance is enhanced by home-grown salads.

Salmon is equally good poached, grilled or baked. There is an old saying that fresh salmon should be cooked 'before it has lost a tide'. The creamy substance between the flakes, which is called the curd, is then at its best, rendering the flesh of the fish more digestible and nourishing than when a few days old.

Boiled salmon is probably the most popular method of cooking the fish, and is delicious hot or cold. Remember that you will need to cover your fish with *boiling* salted water to which a tea-spoonful of lemon juice or wine vinegar has been added, but that the salmon should not boil after that. The water should be kept at the 'shivering' stage of simmering.

Keep in mind, too, that salmon is of such close texture, and so rich in fat, that a little goes a long way.

Some people prefer to boil salmon in *Court Bouillon* rather than acidulated water. Here, is the method for making it.

Court Bouillon

To each quart of water allow:

2 tsps. salt	1 small onion
1 celery stick	½ leek, if available
6 peppercorns	Small piece of turnip
1 wineglass white wine or	Bouquet garni
½ glass wine vinegar	1 carrot

Put enough water in your cooking vessel to cover the salmon to be cooked. Bring to the boil, add the prepared vegetables and simmer for 30 minutes. Meanwhile, wash, clean and pre-pare the piece of salmon. It is a good idea to tie it loosely in a piece of butter muslin for cooking. In this manner, it is easily lifted from the hot liquor.

Skim any scum from the court bouillon before lowering the fish. Boil *very gently* allowing *about* 10 minutes per pound. The larger the piece the less minutes are needed per pound. For instance, a two-pound piece, which would be ample for 4–5 people, will probably be done in half an hour or a trifle under, but a really large portion of salmon, say, eight pounds, will only need about one hour for its cooking time.

Drain well, before serving, and garnish with cucumber. Serve with *Sauce Hollandaise* or anchovy, shrimp, lobster, oyster or parsley sauce. Hot melted butter can be sent to the table as well, if your guests are not slimming.

Salmon steaks, of course, can be cooked in the same fashion, or grilled or baked. Try:

Baked Salmon Steaks

1 salmon steak (about an inch thick) per person.
Chopped shallot, parsley, lemon juice and butter or
vegetable oil.

Butter a baking dish. Place the steaks in the dish and brush
lightly with oil or dot with a very little butter. Sprinkle with
finely chopped shallot, parsley, pepper and salt, cover and cook
in a brisk oven for 10–15 minutes.

Anchovy, caper or tomato sauce goes well with this dish.

Eliza Acton's Salmon Pudding

To be served hot or cold

The great cook adds beneath the title: 'A Scotch Receipt –
Good'.

'Pound or chop small, or rub through a sieve one pound of
cold boiled salmon freed entirely from bone and skin; and blend
it lightly but thoroughly with half a pound of fine breadcrumbs, a
teaspoonful of anchovy essence, a quarter of a pint of cream, a
seasoning of salt and cayenne, and four well-whisked eggs. Press
the mixture closely and evenly into a deep dish or mould, buttered in every part, and bake it for one hour in a moderate oven.

Salmon, 1 lb, breadcrumbs ½ lb, essence of anchovies, 1
teaspoonful; cream, ¼ pint; eggs 4, salt and cayenne; baked
1 hour.'

Here is a more modern recipe for using up cold cooked salmon. It is particularly light and economical, and very suitable for a summer dish.

Salmon Mould

¾ lb cooked salmon or 1 tin   ½ oz or 3 tsps. gelatine
1 hard-boiled egg   Pepper and salt and a few
1 firm tomato   drops of lemon juice

Dissolve gelatine in a cupful of tepid fish stock or water. Mix with flaked fish.

Put slices of hard-boiled egg and tomato at the base and sides of a wetted pudding basin so that the mould will be prettily decorated when it is turned out.

Season the fish with salt, pepper and lemon juice, and press into the basin. Put in the refrigerator to set.

Serve with plenty of cucumber on a bed of lettuce. New potatoes are delicious with this. Rémoulade sauce makes a pleasant change from mayonnaise here.

Pressed Beef

Here is an economical way of dealing with a piece of beef.

3 lb salted or fresh brisket
2 onions
2 carrots
½ oz gelatine
⅓ pint stock

Soak the beef, if salted, for several hours to remove excess salt. Change the water once or twice.

Put it with the sliced vegetables into a large saucepan, cover with water and simmer until meat is tender, about 2 hours.

Transfer meat to a straight-sided tin, such as a cake tin, and press down firmly. Dissolve the gelatine in a little tepid water, then make up to half a pint with hot stock. When the gelatine has thoroughly dissolved, pour over the meat, cover, and stand in a cold larder. A weight on top will ensure a good shape. Turn out when cold and serve with salad.

Pork and Peach Kebabs

1 lb pork fillet
2 oz button mushrooms
1 green pepper, de-seeded
Large tin peach halves

Cut the pork into small cubes. Skin the mushrooms and take off the stalks. Cut the pepper into neat pieces. Blanch both mushrooms and pepper.

Drain the juice from the peach halves and reserve for the sauce.

Now thread these ingredients in turn on to long skewers. Brush all with oil and place under a moderate grill. Baste often, and turn the skewers for even cooking.

Peach Sauce

¼ pint peach juice
¼ pint water
Juice of a lemon

1 dessertsp. soy sauce
Salt and pepper
1 tab. cornflour

Heat the peach juice, water, lemon juice, and soy sauce together. Mix cornflour with a little juice and water to make a paste. Pour the hot liquid into this then return all to the saucepan to cook for 5 minutes, stirring continuously. Season to taste when sauce is thick.

Serve this sauce separately. The kebabs should be served on a bed of hot rice.

Pineapple can be substituted for peaches. Some people may prefer the astringency of this fruit to the sweetness of the peaches.

Baked Gammon with Pineapple

This is always popular, and is equally good hot or cold. Gammon cooked by this method has more flavour and keeps its shape rather better than when it is boiled.

2–3 lb middle cut of gammon
Pork dripping or lard for cooking
1 small tin pineapple rings
A little Barbados or Demerara sugar and a few cloves

Soak the gammon for about 2 hours to remove excessive saltiness. Wrap it in foil and cook in a moderate oven for an hour. Remove foil and take off the skin.

Now put lard or pork dripping into the pan. Score the fat of the gammon into diamonds. Press brown sugar into the scored surface, and press a clove into each diamond. Return to the pan and bake for a further 30 minutes, basting with the fat.

About 10 minutes before dishing up, slip the pineapple rings into the same dish to heat.

Serve the gammon, garnished with the pineapple rings, with a green salad. Potatoes, baked in their jackets, go very well with this dish.

Gammon Rashers with Mushroom Stuffing

Allow 1 ¼-inch thick gammon rasher for each person.
The stuffing needs:

4 oz mushrooms	2 egg yolks
3 oz breadcrumbs	Juice of ½ lemon
1 oz butter	Salt and pepper

Sauté chopped mushrooms in the butter until soft, then add the breadcrumbs, lemon juice and seasoning. Beat the egg yolks and blend into the mixture.

Grill the rashers on both sides.

Now spread the stuffing over the rashers, and grill more gently, basting with the juices, until this coating is browned. Top each rasher with one whole cooked mushroom, and serve very hot.

Ham Timbales

This is a good way of using up the remains of a ham-bone. I have also made timbales with the remains of a chicken. They are deliciously light, and invalids will often eat them when they refuse other forms of the same meat. I cook mine in castle pudding tins. They turn out most attractively and are equally good hot or cold.

½ lb minced ham
2 eggs
4 tabs. white breadcrumbs
6 tabs. milk
Salt and pepper

Warm the milk and add beaten eggs, fine soft breadcrumbs, the minced ham, and mix well. Season to taste. Butter your individual moulds and put the mixture in two-thirds full as it tends to swell during cooking. Stand the moulds in a bain-marie and bake in a moderate oven for about 30 minutes. Serve hot with tomato purée or cold with a green salad.

If you make the timbales with chicken, try adding some freshly chopped parsley to the mixture.

Ham Mousse

1 lb lean ham
½ pt. Béchamel sauce
2 oz butter
Salt, paprika, nutmeg

½ oz powdered gelatine
¼ pint white stock (preferably chicken)
Gill cream

Mince ham finely twice. Work in the mixer, or pound by hand, with the creamed butter and cold Béchamel sauce.

Dissolve gelatine in warmed stock, and whilst still lukewarm, add to the mixture.

Partially whip the cream. It should not be too stiff. Fold into the other ingredients, put into a soufflé dish, and chill.

If desired, the top can be decorated with sliced tomatoes or olives, and glazed over with a little of the gelatine.

Pretty, light, and a perfect summer dish.

Lamb Kebabs

1 lb fillet of lamb
4 shallots or little onions
Aubergine (if liked)
8 button mushrooms

4 small tomatoes
8 rashers
Butter or olive oil for cooking

Cut the meat into cubes of about 1 inch. Partly boil the onions or shallots for about 10 minutes. Skin the mushrooms and tomatoes. Roll up the rashers, and if they are rather large, halve them lengthwise before doing this. Slice the aubergine into ½-inch circles.

Now thread your delicious snippets on 4 skewers. Brush plentifully with melted butter or oil, and cook under a moderate grill, taking care to turn and baste frequently.

If you lodge the skewers on the grill-pan, the surplus fat can be used for basting and the whole operation will be clean and tidy.

The kebabs are good with hot rice and a green salad. I hear that avocado pears cut in half make a luxurious accompaniment to this dish.

Here is a slightly different way of preparing lamb or mutton kebabs.

Kebabs à l'Indienne

8 slices of lamb or mutton	Ground ginger
8 pieces of lean bacon or ham	Curry powder
2 apples	1 oz butter
2 onions	Curry sauce

Core and pare the apples. Skin the onions. Cut apples and onions into 8 slices, and trim the bacon and the lamb or mutton pieces to fit exactly – about 2 inches across.

Sprinkle the meat with a little curry powder, ground ginger and salt.

Thread your pieces, as before, on 4 skewers, brush with melted butter, or olive oil, and cook under the grill.

Serve with rice and curry sauce.

Here is an unusual recipe for mutton from Eliza Acton. It is called:

'China Chilo

Mince a pound of undressed loin or leg of mutton, with or without a portion of its fat; mix with it 2 or 3 young lettuces shred small, a pint of young peas, a teaspoonful of salt, half as much pepper, 4 tablespoonfuls of water, from 2 to 3 ounces of good butter, and, if the flavour be liked, a few green onions minced.

Keep the whole well-stirred with a fork over a clear and gentle fire until it is quite hot, then place it closely covered by the side of the stove, or on a high trivet, that it may stew as softly as possible for a couple of hours. One or even two half-grown cucumbers, cut small by scoring the ends deeply as they are sliced, or a quarter of a pint of minced mushrooms may be added with good effect; or a dessertspoonful of currie powder and a large chopped onion. A dish of boiled rice should be sent to the table with it.

Mutton, 1 pound; green peas, 1 pint; young lettuce, 2; salt; 1 teaspoonful; pepper, $\frac{1}{2}$ teaspoonful; water, 4 tablespoonful; butter, 2–3 ounces; 2 hours.

Varieties: cucumbers 2, or mushrooms minced, $\frac{1}{4}$ pint; or currie powder, 1 dessertspoonful, and 1 large onion.'

I give this recipe in full because it can be so easily adapted to our present-day cookers, and it supplies so many excellent flavours for use with mutton or lamb, which may spark off further ideas of your own.

Individual Lamb Salad

$\frac{1}{2}$–$\frac{3}{4}$ lb cooked lamb
4 globe artichokes
Juice of a lemon
Capers
Mayonnaise

Wash artichokes thoroughly and cook in boiling salted water, to which a squeeze of lemon juice has been added until tender – if young, about 20 minutes should be long enough. Drain and cool them, and carefully pull out the centre leaves, so that only a rim of two or three leaves remains. Remove hairy centre.

Blend diced or minced lamb with a little mayonnaise and a few capers and fill the central cavity of each artichoke. A sprinkling of paprika will improve the look of the filling.

The central leaves can be served separately in another dish dressed with mayonnaise.

This makes a pretty dish for a summer lunch.

Summer Chicken with Peas

1 medium or 2 small spring chickens
2 oz butter

For the peas:

1 lb fresh shelled peas, or	Gill water
2 8-oz packets of frozen	6 sugar knobs
1 cos lettuce	2 oz butter
A few spring onions	Pepper and salt

Melt the butter in a large casserole. Brown the chickens, turning them occasionally in the butter. Cover the casserole and cook in a moderate oven for about an hour.

Shell the peas, or open your packets, and trim the spring onions. Put water, sugar and seasoning into a good-sized saucepan so that the liquor does not boil over, and bring to the boil.

Put in the peas, lettuce, onions and butter. Cover, and simmer gently until cooked. Pour over the chickens, re-cover, and continue to cook for a further three quarters to one hour.

Serve the chickens sliced with their delicious sauce about them.

Pollo Tonnato

This is a simple but unusual way of serving cold chicken. You will need:

1 cooked chicken, or part of one	1 lemon
1 tin tunny	1 tsp. capers
3 anchovies	Olive oil

Cut fairly large pieces from the chicken, and leave on one side.

Prepare the sauce by blending lemon juice, tunny, anchovies and capers until smooth. Gradually add olive oil, beating the while, until a thick sauce is made.

Coat the chicken pieces with this and arrange on a dish garnished with lemon slices and watercress.

Serve the rest of the sauce in a sauceboat.

Jack Rabbit

Here is a useful supper or light lunch dish, using ingredients readily available. It is a mixture of Welsh Rabbit and Scrambled Egg, very savoury and sustaining.

4 oz Cheddar cheese	Lemon juice
2 eggs	Worcester sauce
About 1 wineglass beer	Cayenne pepper

Melt the butter in a saucepan with all the ingredients except the eggs. Stir while the cheese is melting and absorbing the beer and other flavours.

Now beat the two eggs and tip into the mixture. Cook, stirring, until thick over a low heat.

Spread thickly on hot buttered toast, and brown under a brisk grill before bringing it, piping hot, to the table.

Sweets

The traditional time to have one's first dish of gooseberries is Whitsuntide. At one time they were cheap and plentiful. Almost every country garden had its gooseberry bushes ranging from hard green globes of fruit to red prickly ones – almost beery in flavour when really ripe. Then, of course, there were the huge golden dessert gooseberries, tender-skinned and sweet, popping gloriously in the mouth. Where have they all gone?

Parson Woodforde often mentions gooseberries. On May 18 in 1779 some friends came to dinner, and after 'Maccarel, 3 young Chicken boiled and some Bacon, a neck of Pork rosted,' they had 'a Gooseberry Pye hot.'

He goes on to say:

'We laughed immoderately after dinner on Mrs Howes's being sent to Coventry by us for an Hour. What with laughing and eating hot Gooseberry Pye brought on me the Hickupps with a violent pain in my stomach which lasted till I went to bed.'

Here are a few lighter recipes for gooseberries. The first is very simple but you will need really ripe dessert gooseberries to make it successfully.

Gooseberry Cream 1

1 lb ripe dessert gooseberries
1 tab. caster sugar
Gill of cream
Juice of half a lemon

Press ripe gooseberries through a sieve to extract all the pulp and juice. Add sugar and lemon juice and stir together.

Whip cream stiffly and fold it into the mixture. Chill thoroughly for at least an hour, before putting it into individual glasses.

Gooseberry Cream 2

This makes a rather firmer mixture which can be turned out of a mould. Any fruit, turned first into a purée, can be used in this way to make a Fruit Cream which is always popular.

½ pint puréed gooseberries
½ pint thick custard
2 tabs. caster sugar

½ oz gelatine
½ cupful water
½ pint double cream

Sieve the fresh gooseberries as in the first recipe and mix with the custard which should be cold. Add sugar.

Dissolve the gelatine in tepid water, and then heat. When really hot pour it into the mixture and stir well until it begins to feel tacky.

Now fold in the whipped cream and pour into a mould to set. Allow at least 2 hours for it to set perfectly.

Gooseberries, particularly when young, blend well with other flavours. Most people know that elder-flowers improve the flavour of gooseberry jelly. But perhaps the combination of gooseberries with orange has not come your way. Here is a recipe worth trying. Fresh dessert gooseberries are ideal, but bottled ones will do very well.

Gooseberry and Orange Pudding

1 lb gooseberries
1 orange
1 oz butter

4 oz brown sugar
1 egg
4 oz white breadcrumbs

Simmer the gooseberries in about ½ pint of water with half the sugar. Allow to cool.

Melt the butter in a saucepan, grate the orange rind into it, and squeeze in the juice.

Beat gooseberries to a smoothish pulp with a fork, add the beaten egg and tip in the butter, rind and juice. Mix well together.

Well butter a fireproof round dish. Mix the rest of the sugar with the breadcrumbs and press a lining of this mixture to the bottom and sides of the dish. Keep back about half for the top.

Spoon in the gooseberry mixture without disturbing the crumb lining. Sprinkle the rest thickly on top, cover with foil, and bake in a moderate oven for an hour. Remove foil for the last 10 minutes to allow top to brown. This is equally good hot or cold with cream.

Serve from the dish, if hot, but this pudding should turn out quite successfully when really cold.

Junket

Junket is so simple and quick to make and the recipe so readily available that it may seem pointless to mention it. I do so, though, because it is a sweet which is very easily overlooked among the welter of similar milk puddings.

I find that it is cheaper to buy a bottle of plain rennet essence (I use Burgess's) and flavour it as I wish.

These quantities make enough for 4 people.

> 1 pint fresh milk
> 1 dessertsp. caster sugar
> 1–2 tsps. rennet
> Flavouring

Warm the milk to blood heat. Stir in the sugar and add the rennet. Let it set at room temperature. It can be chilled just before serving, if preferred.

Serve with a jugful of single cream, or with stewed fruit as well, and eat the junket the same day as it is prepared.

Most people will agree that by far the best way of eating strawberries is to pick them from a sun-warmed bed, add a dollop of fresh cream and caster sugar, and bask in bliss. Any other method seems almost sacrilegious, but here are a few recipes you may like to try at strawberry time.

Fresh Strawberry Ice Cream

1 lb strawberries
½ pint single cream
6 oz caster sugar
3 egg yolks
½ cupful water

Sieve, or use the electric blender, to reduce the hulled strawberries to a purée. Add 3 oz of the sugar and stir.

Put the rest of the sugar and water in a saucepan, over a low heat. When sugar has dissolved, increase heat and boil for 5 minutes.

Whisk the 3 egg yolks in a basin and gradually pour hot syrup on to them. Whisk well until it thickens.

Now whisk in fruit purée and the cream. Stir all together and put into a dish which fits into the freezing compartment of the refrigerator. Leave for 2–3 hours, or until almost firm, then scoop out again into the basin for another whisking. This is necessary to break down the forming ice crystals.

The final result should be creamy in texture. Refreeze until firm. This will take about another 2 hours.

Strawberry Cream

1 lb strawberries
3 tabs. caster sugar, vanilla-flavoured
¼ pint double cream
¼ pint single cream

Mash the strawberries with a fork and mix with the sugar. Whisk double cream until fairly thick, then add the single cream so that the mixture is not too heavy.

Blend cream and strawberries together and put into individual glasses or one large dish. Decorate with a few whole strawberries.

Strawberry Flan

For flan pastry:

8 oz plain flour
5 oz butter
2 oz caster sugar
2 egg yolks

Cream butter and sugar, sieve in flour, then add beaten egg yolks to mix. A little cold water may also be needed to get a consistency which will roll out well.

Line flan tin, and bake blind.

Pack the hulled strawberries tightly and neatly into the flan case. Three-quarters of a pound should fill an 8-inch case. Cover with this simple glaze:

Melt 4 oz of red-currant jelly and sweeten with 1 tab. caster sugar. A dessertspoon of orange liqueur, such as grand marnier, adds to the flavour.

Pour gently over the strawberries and allow to cool. Serve flan with cream in a separate dish.

Strawberries blend well with other fruit flavourings. Try orange juice squeezed over a dish of fresh strawberries or a few drops of orange liqueur. Dust well with icing sugar and leave to macerate for at least an hour before serving.

Strawberries and raspberries can be mixed together, dredged with icing sugar and served chilled.

And fresh sliced peaches and strawberries make a dish which looks as beautiful as it tastes.

Strawberry Boats

These always look attractive and are equally good as a sweet course or at tea-time.

Line boat-shaped tins with flan pastry (see Strawberry Flan for recipe) and bake blind.

Fill them, when cold, with a row of well-shaped strawberries covered with a mixture of melted red-currant jelly and raspberry jam.

Raspberry Flummery

> 2 raspberry jellies
> 1 lb stewed sweetened raspberries
> or 1 tin raspberries
> 1 large tin evaporated milk

Melt one jelly with a little of the raspberry juice, and make up to 1 pint with water.

Put raspberries into a deep bowl or bowls and pour the jelly over them. Put aside to set.

Melt the second jelly in not more than $\frac{1}{4}$ pint of raspberry juice. Whisk the evaporated milk until it is four or five times its volume. Carefully drip in the melted jelly as you whip the milk.

Pour over the set jelly and raspberries and chill well before serving.

These quantities make a generous amount, and you may find it useful to divide the dish between two bowls.

Other fruits make equally attractive Flummery. Pineapple is particularly refreshing.

Summer Pudding

This old favourite can be delicious if cooked properly, and is most useful when one has a handful of this or that fruit available, but not enough of any one kind to make a satisfying dish. It is the combination of fruits which gives Summer Pudding its distinctive flavour.

Here are two methods:

Stew available fruit, such as red-currants, raspberries, rhubarb and loganberries altogether, with the minimum of water and plenty of white sugar.

Line a wetted pudding basin with slices of white bread from which the crusts have been removed. Put in the fruit, add a lid of bread slices, pressed down well, cover with greaseproof paper or foil and steam for 20 minutes.

This can be eaten hot, with cream, or left to cool with a weighted saucer on top, for eating cold later.

An uncooked version made with sponge cakes, is also very good. You will need:

> 12 individual sponge cakes
> 3–4 oz caster sugar
> 1½ lb–2 lb available fruit

Line a pudding basin with split sponge cakes, and put in the stewed fruit with plenty of sugar. Make sure there is not too much liquid.

Cover with a lid of split sponge cakes, and press well down. Put a weighted saucer on top and leave in a cold place for several hours.

Turn out and serve with cream.

Some people like to coat this pudding with a fruit sauce made by thickening the fruit juice with arrowroot. If you want to do this, you will find that one teaspoonful of arrowroot to half a pint of fruit juice will be about right.

Frosted Red Currants

Pick well-shaped bunches of ripe red-currants.

Whip the white of one egg and with a pastry brush paint the currants with the froth.

Put a heap of caster sugar on a plate and roll the dipped clusters this way and that in the sugar until they are coated.

Dry on a rack at room temperature, and use either in individual glass bowls, or as a decoration on top of a light sponge dusted well with icing sugar, or as a decorative and pleasantly tart addition to a dish of meringues.

Fresh Apricot Mousse

This is simple, rich and delicious.

> 1 lb fresh apricots
> 6 oz icing sugar
> 1 pint double cream

Put the apricots into a basin and cover with boiling water. After a few minutes, peel, cut in half and remove stones.

Rub the fruit through a sieve into another bowl, and add sifted icing sugar as you go. Test for sweetness – you may find that you like less sugar than the 6 oz given. It depends on the ripeness of the apricots, but they can be surprisingly sharp.

Whisk cream until thick and blend with the apricots. Put into the dish in which it will come to the table and chill well.

One or two apricot kernels, skinned, make a suitable decoration. A little Kirsch can be added to the blended cream and apricots, if liked.

Melon Dishes

Melon is less used for a sweet these days because, I suppose, it serves as such a useful and decorative first course, but here are one or two suggestions.

Cut the melon in half lengthways, remove pips and pith. Carefully scoop out the flesh, and dice this, adding small colourful fruit such as stoned cherries, raspberries, sliced bananas, diced pineapple and so on, and fill the two melon shells with the fruit mixture. A little sugar should be sprinkled on the fruit as one is filling the cases.

Try chopped melon with diced preserved ginger and lychees. Serve this mixture in individual glasses, and use a little of the ginger syrup to moisten the dish.

Or, stunning in its simplicity, cut the top off a large and handsome melon – a cantaloup is really the most decorative – scoop out the flesh and chop it neatly into cubes.

Return it to the case, squeezing a little lemon juice and sprinkling castor sugar as you fill. Put on its lid (the slice which was first cut off) and chill before serving.

Cakes

Idiot Biscuits

(So-called, so my friend tells me, because any idiot can make them.)

4 oz butter	4 oz plain flour
2 oz caster sugar	1 tab. cocoa powder
	½ tsp. vanilla essence

Cream fat and sugar together and add essence. Stir in flour and cocoa. Roll into small balls and place on a greased baking sheet. Press down a little with a fork dipped in hot water, and bake in a moderate oven for about 20–30 minutes.

Victorian Orange Buns

These are unusual and always liked.

4 oz flour	4 oz caster sugar
½ tsp. baking powder	2 eggs
4 oz butter	Grated rind of 1 large orange and its juice

Cream butter and sugar. Add grated orange rind and beaten eggs, and lastly sift in the flour and baking powder.

Moisten with the orange juice and beat well. The mixture should be like that of a sponge cake.

Divide into bun cases, and cook in a fairly hot oven for 12-15 minutes.

Strawberry Jam

To my mind, this is the finest of all jams, but it can be the very deuce to make satisfactorily. There must be gallons and gallons of strawberry jam made in English kitchens each summer which 'turns out runny.'

In one useful cookery book I have there are lists of fruit given which are rich or deficient in pectin – that magic substance which determines whether a jam sets easily or not. Strawberries appear in the 'deficient in pectin' list, and it is absolutely essential to add lemon juice or red-currant juice to ensure success.

Hull the strawberries, wash, drain and weigh them, and allow 1 lb preserving sugar to each pound.

Put fruit and sugar in layers in a large bowl and leave overnight in a cool place.

Put into a preserving pan next day with the juice of 4 lemons, or ½ pint of red-currant juice.

Bring slowly to the boil, stirring very gently. Strawberries damage very easily.

Boil rapidly for about 30 minutes, skimming frequently, and test for a set on a cold plate.

Allow jam to cool slightly in the pan before pouring it into the warmed jars. This ensures that the fruit is adequately spaced, otherwise it rises to the top.

Fresh Apricot Jam

You will need to buy 3½ lb of apricots for the recipe below needs 3 lb when stoned. It makes the loveliest golden preserve and keeps well.

> 3 lb fresh apricots
> 3 lb preserving sugar
> Juice of 2 lemons
> Gill of water

Halve apricots and remove stones. Keep a few kernels to add to the finished jam.

In a large bowl put layers of apricots and preserving sugar until all are used. Finish with a sugar layer, and leave in a cool place until the next day.

Now put water and lemon juice in a large saucepan, add fruit and sugar and bring to the boil *very slowly*. Make sure that the sugar has melted, then simmer for about 30–40 minutes, stirring occasionally.

Test for setting, and allow jam to cool slightly before potting. Add blanched and halved kernels halfway through the simmering.

Mint Jelly

This home-made jelly has more tang than the bought variety. As you see, this recipe uses apples, but I have made it with green gooseberries, in the same way, and it turned out quite successfully.

2 lb cooking apples
2 pints water
1 lb preserving sugar to each strained pint

Fresh mint sprigs
Green colouring
Juice of 1 lemon

Wash apples, chop roughly and put in a preserving pan with the water and lemon juice. Simmer for about 20 minutes. Put into a jelly bag and strain overnight.

Now allow 1 lb of sugar to each pint of strained liquid, return to pan, let sugar dissolve and then boil for 5 minutes.

Keep a few sprigs of mint on one side for later chopping. Put the bulk in a clean muslin bag and immerse in the boiling jelly. Ten minutes should be enough, then drain the bag and throw it away.

When the jelly sets, draw it away from heat whilst you chop the mint. Cover with boiling water and let it stand for about 5 minutes to draw out the flavour. Drain and add to the jelly.

Now add very cautiously a few drops of green colouring matter until it pleases your eye. Stir and then put in small jars.

If you prefer a clear jelly, omit the chopped mint, but it certainly adds more flavour.

These quantities make about 3 lb of jelly.

Autumn

There is something decidedly satisfying about the coming of Autumn. It is a time to clear up the garden, to burn the brittle bean sticks, to pull up the dying annuals, and to garner those poor green tomatoes before the frost annihilates them.

In the fields the harvest is being collected. The combines chug round like prehistoric monsters. The grain dryers hum from vast farm buildings, and country women are busy, too, picking apples, plums and pears and filling bottling jars and jam-pots as well as the deep-freezer.

There is a cosiness about, the feeling which Kanga had one day when she wanted to count Roo's vests and the tablets of soap in the store cupboard. If the summer has been cold, it is a positive relief to welcome Autumn fires and early nights.

Stacking logs, storing apples, fetching another blanket for the bed, give us a comfortable feeling of rare efficiency in our preparations for Winter. It is a time for looking forward and cooks, in particular, have plenty of autumnal delights to challenge their skill. Wild fruits abound in the hedgerow, sloes, crab-apples and blackberries. Stone fruit, apples and pears are ready for her ministrations, and game of all sorts comes into season. It is, perhaps, the most exciting of all the seasons for the cook who has the time and energy to make use of Autumn's almost embarrassing bounty.

Soups

Game Purée

The remains of pheasant, grouse, partridge or hare make a delicious soup. The more meat on them the better.

Carcase of one of the above	1 tab. red-currant, rowan or
1 carrot	gooseberry jelly
1 onion	½ glass of port or Burgundy
Bouquet of herbs	2 pints stock

Simmer carcase in the stock with vegetables and herbs, until meat is easily flaked from the bone and vegetables are soft. When cool remove meat and pass it through a sieve or mill into a clean saucepan. Add strained liquor in which it has cooked, then the red-currant jelly, wine and seasoning. Simmer for a further 5 minutes. Serve with croûtons.

Marrow Soup

This is worth remembering when you are presented with your fourth marrow in one Autumn week by kind neighbours.

1 small marrow	2 oz cornflour
1 onion	1½ pints milk
2 oz butter	½ pint white stock or water

Peel the marrow, remove seeds and cut into slices. Put it, with chopped onion, into a saucepan, cover with stock and simmer gently until soft. Put through a sieve and add the milk to the resultant purée. In another saucepan, melt the butter, stir in cornflour and allow to thicken. Add the purée very gradually, stirring the whole until it comes to the boil. Season and simmer for about 8 minutes.

A little cream, about 2 tablespoons, can be added just before serving. Make sure that soup is not boiling at this stage and does not boil after the addition of cream.

Serve with croûtons, or sprinkle finely chopped tarragon on top.

Tapioca Cream Soup

I first tasted this delicious old-fashioned soup at Urchfont Manor in Wiltshire. It was as elegant and unusual as the Abyssinian cat which wins the affection of all those who visit this lovely old house when attending courses – not culinary ones, but academic and practical, I mean. Don't be put off by childhood memories of 'white frogs' spawn'. It is a bland, easily-digested soup, very comforting, and perfect for invalids.

> 1 oz crushed tapioca or semolina
> 2 egg yolks
> ½ pint milk
> 1 quart white stock

Boil up stock, skimming scum. Add tapioca or semolina, and stir until transparent. Beat egg yolks in a basin and add the milk to them. Pour a little hot stock into this mixture and stir well. Return all to saucepan, season, and stir till soup thickens. Do not allow it to boil. Sprinkle with chopped parsley or chives.

Mushroom Soup

If you are fortunate enough to have field mushrooms growing nearby then this recipe will be even more rewarding than if you have to buy the cleaner, neater, but rather less tasty variety from the shop. I think that finding mushrooms in dewy grass is almost as exciting as finding warm new-laid eggs in an old-fashioned nest-box rustling with yellow straw. One never grows too old to enjoy such simple pleasures, I find.

4 oz mushrooms	Salt and pepper
1 small onion	2 pints of good white stock
1 oz butter	⅛ pint thin cream
1 oz cornflour	

Sauté the chopped onion in butter until it is transparent. Add chopped mushrooms and cook gently for 5 minutes till all is blended with the butter. Add stock and seasoning. Simmer for 20 minutes.

Put through mill or sieve and return to saucepan. Blend cornflour with 2 tablespoons of cold stock, add some hot liquid carefully to the mixture. Return to pan stirring continuously until the soup thickens. Add cream, taking care that the soup is not boiling, just before serving. Grated Parmesan cheese is good with this soup, but serve separately, as some people dislike it melting into the hot liquid.

Veal Broth

This is a meal in itself, light and nourishing.

Small knuckle of veal	A bouquet of herbs
4 oz rice	4 pints water
2 onions	Salt and pepper
Shred of lemon peel	

Wash knuckle and put in saucepan with cold water. Bring slowly to the boil and remove scum. The addition of a little salt and a spoonful of cold water helps the scum to rise at this stage. Simmer for 1 hour, then add washed rice, salt, pepper, bouquet garni, and the onions and lemon peel. Simmer for another 1½ hours. Remove knuckle, and arrange meat in pieces in heated tureen. Remove lemon peel and bouquet. Add liquor including rice and onions, to the tureen and serve very hot. Small-diced toast can accompany this dish.

Iced Vichyssoise

It is the leeks which give this soup its distinctive flavour, which is why you find this cold soup recipe under the Autumn heading. It is an elegant first course, and if your central heating works well then why not have an iced dish first instead of last?

1 lb leeks
1 lb potatoes
1 oz butter
2 pints chicken stock

½ cup cream
1 tab. chopped chives
Salt and pepper

Remove all green part of leeks. Shred the white finely. Peel and chop potatoes into dice. Melt butter in a saucepan, add leeks and potatoes and cook gently for 10 minutes. Add stock and seasoning and simmer for 30–40 minutes. Cool and rub through sieve. Add cream when purée is cold. Chill, and sprinkle with chives when serving.

Almond and Celery Soup

Head of celery
1 small onion
3 oz sweet almonds
1½ pints white stock

½ pint milk
Salt and pepper
1 oz flour and 1 oz butter for roux

Chop inner part of celery, onion and almonds, and simmer altogether in the stock for at least an hour. Rub through sieve.

Make the roux with flour and butter, add the purée of vegetables, stirring the while, then the milk. Bring to the boil, still stirring.

Remove from heat and add a few shredded toasted almonds – cream too, if so desired – and serve.

Hors d'oeuvre

Red and Green Peppers

Both red and green peppers make an attractive hors d'oeuvre. Wash, and take out all the seeds. Cut into very fine rounds or strips and mix with a little vinaigrette sauce, made as follows:

> 2 tabs. olive oil
> 1 tab. white wine vinegar
> Pinch of salt, sugar and pepper

Olives go well with peppers and improve the look of this dish.

Avocado Pear

For the purist the only way to serve an avocado pear is to cut it in half, remove the stone, and fill the hole with vinaigrette sauce. But recently I heard of another way of turning an avocado pear into an interesting, and rather rich, dish which you may like to try.

Half an avocado for each person
1 small dessertsp. game pâté for each
Sour cream
Salt and pepper

Peel the pears and remove stones. Fill the hole with the pâté and place cut side down on the dish. Cover lightly with sour cream seasoned with salt and pepper. A sprinkling of paprika improves the look of this dish.

Stuffed Tomatoes

Choose large, ripe, but firm tomatoes, and allow one for each person. Slice the top off and take out the seeds. Sprinkle a little salt inside and drain after a few minutes.

Here are some suggested fillings:

(1) Cream cheese blended with the tomato pulp and a pinch of basil or, alternatively, curry powder.

(2) Chopped shrimps with the pulp, basil, and a little thick cream.

(3) Flaked cooked crab, instead of shrimps.

(4) Yolk of hard-boiled eggs mixed with anchovy sauce.

Arranged on young lettuce leaves this makes a colourful first course. Thinly sliced radishes make an attractive garnish to the dish.

Potted Hare

A friend of mine once left a hare *en casserole* in the slow oven of her Esse overnight by mistake. In the morning, of course, the flesh had fallen away from the bones, the gravy was rich and thick and the vegetables very well done. What could be done about all this goodness? How to turn the gorgeous mess into an attractive dish? The answer is in the recipe below.

Remove the cooked meat carefully and sieve it, or mince *twice*. If the meat has already been seasoned, as in my friend's case, then simply moisten with a little of the good gravy, press into a nice-looking dish and cover the top with a little melted butter.

If you feel that the meat needs more flavouring, add a little powdered mace, basil, or a little garlic, according to taste.

The remains of poultry, game birds and ham can be treated similarly. A little made mustard improves them, and the sieved meat will be of a better consistency if it is blended with enough melted butter to make the mixture malleable before potting it. Cover with melted butter.

These potted meats are really delicious. They are perfect for sandwich making as well as for serving with hot toast as the first course. They will keep safely for several days in a refrigerator.

Stuffed Peppers

Allow one pepper per person. Remove the stalks, seeds and core.

For the filling mix finely shredded carrot, radish and tomato, small-diced cucumber and seasoning, in a good mayonnaise. Some people like a little finely chopped onion added to the mixture.

Fill the empty peppers, and serve on a bed of lettuce.

Potted Beef

Leftovers of good lean cold beef make excellent potted meat.

¾ lb finely minced cooked beef
2 oz butter
Pinch of paprika or marjoram

Melt the butter. Blend in beef and herbs. Press into little pots and cover with a layer of melted butter. Very good with hot toast.

Cooked liver can also be treated in the same way, and makes a very good substitute for pâté. It is improved by a small quantity of cooked bacon or ham mixed with it.

Tomato and Onion Tart

This is a fairly substantial first course and could be used as a light main dish.

Short Pastry

8 oz plain flour
4 oz butter
Pinch of salt

1 egg yolk
1 tsp. lemon juice
Iced water to mix

Rub butter into flour and salt until it has the consistency of fine breadcrumbs. Add beaten egg yolk, then lemon juice. Mix to a soft dough with iced water. Roll into a ball, wrap in foil and let it wait in the refrigerator for at least an hour. Roll out and 'bake blind' in a hot oven. Remove foil and allow to cool.
Prepare the filling:

6 large ripe tomatoes
2 tabs. tomato purée
2 large onions
Anchovy fillets

2 oz butter
3 tabs. olive oil
3 oz grated Parmesan cheese
Pinch tarragon

Peel tomatoes, simmer in the olive oil and tomato purée. In another saucepan cook the sliced onions in the melted butter.

When ingredients of both saucepans are thoroughly soft, blend together with chopped tarragon and the grated cheese.

Put this mixture into the cooked pastry shell, and arrange anchovy fillets in a lattice-work pattern on top. Decorate with black olives, if desired, and brush these and anchovy fillets with a little olive oil before baking for about 20–30 minutes in a moderate oven.

Savoury Croûtons

Here is an unusual mixture but it makes a pleasant change spread on hot toast or croûtons of fried bread.

> 4 oz cooked smoked haddock or kipper fillets
> 1 pickled gherkin
> 1 oz butter

Mince the gherkin and fish together. Season well. A pinch of tarragon helps here. Put the butter and this mixture into a saucepan and heat thoroughly. When hot spread on the toast or croûtons, and serve piping hot.

Stuffed Mushrooms

Allow two decent-sized mushrooms per person. You will also need:

A little finely minced ham, half that quantity of fresh white breadcrumbs, chopped parsley, a knob of butter and milk enough to mix. Some people like a little chopped onion in addition.

Peel the mushrooms and take out stalks. Mix together all the ingredients for the stuffing and spread thickly on the upturned mushrooms. Put a small piece of butter on each. Place in a greased dish and bake for about 15 minutes. Serve on toast or croûtons.

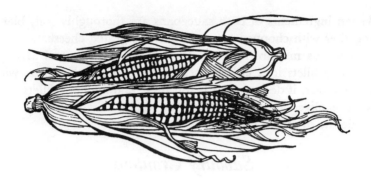

Sweet Corn

Probably the best way to serve this attractive vegetable is in its simplest form – boiled until tender in salted water, drained, and served very hot with hot melted butter, allowing one cob for each person. The time of cooking varies from 10–30 minutes. The kernels can be detached easily when they are done.

Another way to serve sweet corn is to remove the cooked kernels from the cob, mix them in a good white sauce, put them in scallop shells, or any other small individual dishes, sprinkle with a little grated cheese and brown them in the oven.

Cooked sweet corn, or the tinned variety, makes a cheerful addition to a mixed hors d'oeuvre.

Main Dishes

Skate

Skate is a fish which often gets neglected, but many people hold that its flavour is better than that of any other white fish. The wing is the best part of this fish, which belongs to the ray family.

It fries beautifully, but here are a few different ways of cooking this excellent fish which you may like to try. It is at its best in the winter months.

Skate in Cheese Sauce

For 4 people you will need:

1½ lb skate
½ pint white sauce
2 oz grated cheese (Parmesan is best)
2 tabs. breadcrumbs

2 egg yolks
1 oz butter
1 gill cream
½ pint fish stock
Pepper and salt

Cut the skate into neat pieces and simmer in the fish stock until cooked. Add the white sauce, stirring continuously. Then add the cheese, beaten eggs and, away from direct heat, the cream.

Put the mixture in a fireproof dish. Sprinkle breadcrumbs on top, and dot with butter. Put in a hot oven to cook for about 20–30 minutes.

Skate in Cider

2 lb skate
1 oz butter
1 oz flour
3 tabs. cream

½ pint dry cider
1 small onion
1 tab. wine vinegar
Pinch of salt

Cut fish into 4 portions. Put cider, vinegar, sliced onion and salt into a saucepan and bring to the boil. Immerse the skate in this liquid and simmer for about 30 minutes.

Drain, and keep about ½ pint of the liquor for the sauce. Put the fish into a fireproof dish and keep hot.

Melt the butter, thicken with flour, and gradually add the cider liquor. Stir continuously, and cook for a few minutes after thickening.

Remove the pan from heat, stir in cream, pour over the skate and serve immediately.

Lemon or orange wedges, parsley or watercress, make an attractive garnish.

Skate with Orange Butter

Cook the skate as in the receipe above for 'Skate in Cheese Sauce'.

The Orange Butter Sauce is made by heating 2 oz butter, and adding 2 finely-chopped shallots or 1 small onion.

Simmer gently until the shallots or onion are soft. Now add the juice of one orange and a tablespoon of lemon juice.

Season to taste. Simmer for a few minutes and pour over the hot skate pieces. Serve very hot, garnished with orange wedges.

Plaice Mornay

Sole fillets or portions of halibut, haddock or cod, can all be cooked in the same way.

4 fillets of plaice, or other selected fish.

For the sauce you will need:

1 oz butter
1 oz flour
½ pint milk or milk and fish stock mixed

3 oz grated cheese
½ tsp. mustard
½ tsp. grated nutmeg
Salt and pepper

Arrange fish with a little of the milk, in a buttered dish, and bake for about 15 minutes in a moderate oven. Alternatively, steam the fish between two plates over a saucepan for about 10 minutes and then transfer to warm serving dish.

Make the sauce by melting the butter and stirring in the flour. Gradually add the milk, and stir until thick. Add the mustard, nutmeg, salt and pepper to taste.

Now add the cheese, and stir until blended. Coat the fish with the sauce. Brown under the grill for a minute or two, and serve.

Stuffed Plaice Fillets

8 fillets of plaice, 2 per person
4 hard-boiled eggs
1 oz butter

1 oz flour
1 tsp. anchovy essence
¾ pint milk
Pepper and salt

Cut eggs in half, and put one half on each fillet. Sprinkle with salt and pepper, then roll up and put in a fireproof dish.

Make a white sauce with the butter, flour and milk. Add anchovy sauce and seasoning. Pour over fillets and bake in a fairly hot oven for 30 minutes.

Halibut with Chive Butter

4 halibut steaks (turbot will make an equally good dish)
2 oz butter
1 tab. chopped chives
1 tab. lemon juice
Salt and pepper

Melt the butter. Sprinkle the steaks with lemon juice, and then brush with melted butter.

Place them in a greased fireproof dish. Cover, and bake for about 30 minutes in a moderate oven.

Add chopped chives and seasoning to the rest of the melted butter. Pour over the steaks, and serve with lemon wedges.

Grilled Plaice with Cream Cheese

Allow approximately 2 fillets for each person. Grill the fillets on one side, turn them over and spread with soft cream cheese sprinkled with a little lemon juice. Grill this side gently.

Thicker pieces of fish, say cod cutlets, will naturally need longer initial grilling on *both* sides before spreading on the cream cheese. This is a quick and flavoursome dish.

At harvest-time, as the great combines rumble round the cornfields, the country cook begins to look forward to creating game dishes. For, from mid-August onward, the most delectable birds come into season. Please refer to the list 'Game and Poultry in Season' for specific dates.

The question is often asked: 'How long should game be hung?' and to that question there is no fool-proof answer. Remember that the creatures are being hung to render them tender. *Rigor mortis*, the first stage after death, must have passed before the tenderizing period begins. It is sometimes thought that 'gaminess' (or partial putrefaction) is the reason for hanging.

Naturally, a lot depends on the weather. A bird will need less time to hang in warm muggy weather than in cold. Hang it in a cool airy place (mine does well in the back porch which faces north-west), and try to find out when the bird was shot. A pheasant, for instance, should be hung from 5 to 12 days, some would say for up to a fortnight, but as with all game, the length of time depends on the weather, the size and type of bird, and on personal taste.

One hint, though. That popular story of pulling the tail feathers and reckoning the bird ready when they come out easily, is *not infallible*. If you wait that long you *may* discover that the tail feathers are securely attached to a corpse fast turning green. It has been known, so be warned.

There is no nobler dish for a sharp autumn day than a beautiful game pie. Here is a recipe, somewhat extravagant, but producing a magnificent article.

Game Pie

1½ lb raw game flesh (pheasant, partridge, pigeon, or combined)
¾ lb rump steak or veal
¼ lb ham or lean bacon
¼ lb button mushrooms
1 onion
1 oz butter

2 tabs. olive oil
1 tab. mixed chopped parsley and thyme
Salt and black pepper
½ pint stock
Cupful of red wine with a good dash of brandy in it
Flaky pastry for lid

Cut the flesh into neat pieces and marinate in the wine and brandy for about 3 hours.

Cut the veal or steak and the ham into strips and line a deep pie dish. Sprinkle with a little of the finely chopped onions and herbs and a few pieces of the quartered button mushrooms. Season with a little salt and pepper.

Take the game from the marinade and brown the pieces lightly in melted butter and oil. Place them on the bed of meat already in the dish, tuck in any extra pieces of ham, steak or veal, and the rest of the mushrooms. Strew the rest of the herbs on top, and add a little more salt and pepper.

Now use a mixture of the marinade, stock, and juices from the frying-pan to moisten the pie. Line the edges with flaky pastry, and cover with pastry lid. Make a hole in the centre, and if the meat is not sufficiently high in the dish then add a pie funnel to help support the crust.

Gild with beaten egg yolk and decorate with pastry leaves.

It will need a hot oven to begin with, but as soon as the pastry begins to colour, reduce to a moderate heat. If you are afraid the pastry will scorch, then put a piece of foil lightly over it at this stage.

It will take about 1½ hours to cook and will smell divine whilst doing so.

Use stock and wine marinade to make a beautiful gravy.

Pheasant Salmi

This method of cooking can be used for partridge, pigeon and chicken.

1 pheasant	1 tab. red-currant jelly
¾ pint brown stock	4 oz button mushrooms
4 tabs. red wine	2 shallots and a bouquet
2 tabs. port or Madeira	garni

Prepare the bird as if for roasting, but cook for only 15 minutes. Carve it neatly as for the table. Put the pieces into a large casserole or stewpan.

Simmer the carcase in wine and water with a few chopped

shallots or onion, the giblets, and bouquet garni for your brown stock. Add any gravy from the roasting pan to the ¾ pint of stock needed.

To this add the red-currant jelly and Madeira or port. Pour all over the jointed bird, cover and simmer for 30 minutes.

Add sliced mushroom, and cook for a further 15 minutes or until bird is tender.

If you have cooked the bird in a stewpan, then serve on a hot dish with triangles of bread fried in butter. Otherwise, lodge the triangles neatly round the casserole edge and bring to the table.

Of course, young birds are best for this dish, but elderly ones respond very well to this treatment, as both the wine and the slow cooking help to break down toughness.

Pheasant with Apple

This is a useful recipe if you have an elderly bird to cook. It is extremely simple, and rather similar in method to Chicken Stanley.

1 pheasant	¼ lb butter
2 or 3 large cooking apples	Pepper and salt
1 glass red wine, or 4 tabs. stock or water	

Slice the apples and put almost all at the bottom of a deep casserole. The rest put inside the cleaned bird with a lump of butter. Dot the apples with a little butter, and pour in the wine or stock, and seasoning.

Now put the bird on the apple bed and spread it liberally with the rest of the butter. Cover and cook in a moderate oven for about an hour, or just over, depending on the size and age of the bird.

Serve the strained apple separately in a sauceboat and use the excellent juices as gravy.

Friends tell me that celery can be substituted for the apple, or a mixture of both is equally delicious, but I have not yet tried this. I think it would be wise to parboil the celery before using it, as it takes an unconscionable time a-cooking, I always find. Celery hearts, from a tin, should do very well.

Potted Game

Any game birds, rabbit or hare, are excellent potted, and by using different herbs and spices a variety of useful potted meats can be made. For those who have sandwiches to cut daily, these delicious meats are a welcome standby.

Cook the game, rabbit or whatever is available in any way you like. Take the meat from the bone, and mince it very finely (twice, if you can face it) with about a third of its weight in ham fat. If preferred, melt butter of the same amount, i.e. the third of the meat's weight, in a saucepan and blend the minced meat thoroughly with it.

Now add your seasonings. Any types of pepper, allspice, minced onion, crushed garlic, tomato purée, as well as salt, are all suitable. Press the mixture into small moulds, or the old-fashioned stone jam jars if you are lucky enough to have them.

You will need to exclude air by pouring clarified butter to a depth of about a quarter of an inch on top, and cover with a polythene jam pot cover. This mixture will keep safely for several weeks in a cool place, and can be used sliced with salad, or spread on hot toast, as well as making tasty sandwich fillings.

Boiled Partridges

It is good to know that, in some places, partridges are increasing in number after their serious decline. Changes in farming methods had upset their habitual diet. They are at their best in September and October.

Partridges are still pathetically few in this part of the country. Their numbers have never really picked up since the appalling winter of 1962–63 when six partridges lived here in the garden sharing the food scattered for the rest of the starving birds.

As I have said earlier, I do not propose to give the classic recipes, such as roasting, which are well-known, and, without doubt, the finest method of cooking these birds, but here is one of Eliza Acton's sound recipes, which is simple and speedy.

'This is a delicate mode of dressing young and tender birds. Strip off the feathers, clean and wash them well: cut off the heads, truss the legs like those of boiled fowls, and when ready, drop them into a large pan of boiling water; throw a little salt on them, and in 15 or at the utmost in 18 minutes they will be ready to serve.

Lift them out, dish them quickly, and send them to the table with white mushroom sauce, with bread sauce and game gravy, or with celery sauce. Our own mode of having them served is usually with a slice of fresh butter, about a table-spoonful of lemon juice, and a good sprinkling of cayenne placed in a very hot dish, under them.'

Braised Partridge or Pigeon

Allow one bird for 2 people
Onions and carrots
2 oz butter

1 medium-sized crisp cabbage
6 rashers
Pepper and salt and stock

Brown the birds lightly in melted butter. Put a small onion inside each bird with knob of butter.

Place them in a stew pan, or a deep casserole, with sliced carrots and onions. Season well.

Now round the birds tuck the bacon rolls and the cabbage, quartered and blanched. Moisten with a little stock, and simmer for about 1½ hours. This is a good method of cooking toughish birds.

Ducks are equally good braised. You can vary the vegetables by cooking them with buttered young turnips, olives or celery, instead of the onions and carrots.

Daube de Boeuf

This is a tasty dish and the meat is guaranteed to emerge tender. For 4 people you will want:

2–2¼ lb of topside of beef in the piece

6 rashers streaky bacon

3 carrots

3 large tomatoes

3 onions

2 cloves of garlic

Bayleaf

Glass of red wine

2 tabs. olive oil

Salt and pepper

This dish can be cooked in a stewpan on top of the stove or in a casserole in a slow oven.

Put the olive oil to heat in the vessel of your choice. Brown the meat on all sides and put to one side.

Chop bacon, onions, carrots, bay leaf and crushed garlic in the oil, but not the tomatoes. Season well, and put back the meat on top of the vegetables. Pour the wine over all and put a lid on very securely.

Cook very slowly in a low oven for at least 2½ hours. Turn the meat occasionally, and half an hour before dishing up, add the sliced tomatoes.

Serve on a hot dish with the vegetables round it. The gravy should be skimmed, as it will be rather greasy, reheated, and poured round the meat.

Flemish Fillets of Beef

This is expensive, but delicious. It is also extremely simple to prepare and pretty when served.

For 4 people you will need:

1½ lb undercut or fillet of beef	Tab. chopped parsley
2 oz butter	Young carrots
1 pint stock or gravy	2 egg yolks
	Seasoning

Cut the undercut into neat slices about half an inch thick. Trim the slices so that they are similar in shape.

Season them with pepper and salt and dredge with flour. Melt the butter, bring it to a good heat and sauté the slices.

Halve the carrots lengthwise, parboil and drain them. Melt a little butter in a saucepan, put in the carrots seasoned with salt, pepper and a little nutmeg, if liked, toss till well-coated with the butter, then cover with stock or gravy and allow to simmer until tender. Before dishing up, add the beaten yolks of 2 eggs, off the heat.

Arrange the fillets round a serving dish, placing the carrots and thick gravy in the centre. Sprinkle with freshly chopped parsley and serve immediately.

Choice vegetables in season, such as asparagus, peas or French beans make this a memorable feast.

Beef Stroganoff

This is one of those dishes which really needs good well-hung beef. I once tried to make it with a cheaper cut, but it was horribly tough. For 4 servings get:

1½ lb rump or fillet steak
1 onion
2 oz butter
¼ lb button mushrooms
Salt and pepper

3 tomatoes
Glass of white wine
¼ pint fresh double cream
or 2 cartons natural yoghurt

The steak should be cut into slices ½ in. thick, and then cut again into strips about 2 in. by ½ in.

Melt the butter and fry the sliced onion in it, with the steak strips. Cook both for about 8 minutes, turning occasionally. Remove with a slotted spoon, and put sliced mushrooms and tomatoes into the butter to cook for about 3–5 minutes.

Replace steak and onions and season to taste. Gently stir in wine and cream or yoghurt. It *must not boil*, but reheat carefully and cook covered, for a further 15–20 minutes. A dusting of paprika improves the look of this dish.

Serve it with plain rice, boiled potatoes or noodles.

Boiled Silverside

2–3 lb salted silverside of beef	4 carrots
4 small onions	2 young turnips
2 sticks celery	Bouquet garni

Soak the silverside for several hours, changing the water once or twice to get rid of excess salt.

Put into a large saucepan with the bouquet garni and cover with fresh cold water. Bring slowly to the boil and remove scum. Simmer for an hour and a half.

Now add the vegetables, sliced except for the onions, and cook for a further hour.

20 minutes before serving add small *dumplings* made with:

4 oz plain flour
1 tsp. baking powder
2 oz shredded suet
Pinch of salt

These quantities should provide 6–8 dumplings.

Let them simmer for the last 20 minutes of cooking time. Serve meat surrounded by vegetables and dumplings. The gravy should not be thickened, but served separately in a sauce boat. Parsley sauce can also be served with this dish.

Swiss Beef and Onions

This is one of those obliging roasts which needs no attention whilst cooking.

3 lb topside of beef
1 large onion   } or 1 packet of
Teaspoon marjoram } brown onion soup mix

Put the meat on a large piece of foil, sprinkle with finely chopped onion and marjoram, or the soup mix. Wrap completely, making sure the joint is well sealed, and bake in a slow oven for 2½ to 3 hours.

This method ensures a well-flavoured and tender joint.

From Michaelmas to March is traditionally the season for pork, although in these days of deep-freezing we are confident of its goodness all the year round. But years ago, as autumn drew on, the time for the killing of the family pig was welcomed in many cottage homes. Not that joy was the only emotion felt at this time. Flora Thompson describes her own sadnes and horror, as a child, at the pig-sticker's visit, when the friend of the family suddenly became mute and stiff, and hung, a ghastly split corpse, from a hook in the pantry. The rich supper of fried liver could not be faced, although the rest of the family relished this rare delicacy.

Nevertheless, as sorrow faded, the home-killed pig's wholesome flesh was appreciated as the cold weather increased. It did, in fact, constitute the main meat for the year, served in dozens of different ways.

Parson Woodforde notes in his diary on December 7th, 1786:

'Nancy's Pigg was Killed this Morning and a nice, fine, fat White Pigg it is. We are to make some Somersett black Puddings to Morrow, if we can, by our Receipt from thence.'

I wish I could give you Parson Woodforde's Receipt. I feel sure that it would be excellent. However, here is another way of cooking pork, which is perfect for colder days.

Boiled Pork with Pease Pudding

1 small leg or hand of pickled or salted pork	1 stick celery
	1 carrot
1 onion	Salt and pepper
1 small turnip	

Cover joint with cold water, and add the pot vegetables roughly chopped. Simmer for about 2½ hours allowing 25 minutes to the pound, until the joint is done.

Prepare Pease Pudding as follows:

Soak 1 pint of split peas overnight. Drain, transfer to fresh water in a saucepan and simmer for *approximately* an hour and a half.

When soft, sieve them, and add 1 ounce of butter and the beaten yolk of one egg. Season to taste. Blend all together and put the purée into a greased dish covered with foil and steam or bake for a further half an hour.

If you prefer, there are some very good tinned varieties of pease pudding to be bought, which simply need heating.

Pork Cottage Pie

1½ lb minced cooked pork	1 tab. chopped parsley
2 rashers	Stock to moisten
½ onion	Mashed potato to cover

Mince pork, rashers and onion very finely. Sprinkle with parsley, and mix with stock to a fairly wet consistency. Season with salt and pepper.

Mash potatoes with a knob of butter, salt, pepper and a shake of nutmeg. Spread over the meat mixture which is in a shallow fireproof dish, making sure that the edges are well-sealed. Bubbling gravy sometimes discolours the top if gaps are left round the edge.

Bake in a moderate oven for one hour. The top should be golden brown by this time. If not, it may be finally browned under a hot grill.

Hot skinned tomatoes, tomato purée, or braised celery or onions go well with Pork Cottage Pie.

Braised Gammon

Allow a gammon rasher, about ¼ inch thick per person

> 2 apples
> 1 large onion
> 1 oz butter
> Tsp. made mustard

Brown both sides of the gammon rashers and put them in a casserole on a layer of finely sliced onions which you have softened in the melted butter, and the *raw* slices of apple. Cover the rashers with the rest of the sliced onion and apple. Season and moisten with a little stock or water.

Cook in a slow oven for 50–60 minutes. When done, remove rashers and keep warm. Beat the onion and apple together (strain off excess stock if necessary) and to this purée add the teaspoon of made mustard. It is best to serve this sauce separately.

Pork Chops with Apple and Cinnamon

> 4 pork chops
> 2 oz butter
> 2 cooking apples
> Cinnamon
> Pepper and salt

Brown the chops on each side in a little melted butter. Peel and slice the apples. Put a layer in the bottom of a casserole, sprinkle well with cinnamon and seasoning. Put the chops on top, and cover with another layer of apple, seasoning and cinnamon. Finally, dot with butter, cover and cook in a slow oven for an hour.

No moisture is needed. The melted butter, the apples and the steam, cook the chops very tenderly.

Serve the apple and cinnamon separately and choose bland vegetables to go with this rather delicately flavoured dish.

Pork Hot-Pot

1 large potato
1 onion
1 apple
2 lb lean pork

1 tsp. chopped or dried sage
Pepper and salt
Stock or water to cover

Peel the potato, slice fairly thickly and place in the bottom of a casserole. Cut the meat into decent-sized pieces, and arrange in layers with sliced apple and onion, and a sprinkling of sage and seasoning between the layers. Just cover with stock or water.

Place a lid on the casserole, and allow 2 hours in a slow to moderate oven.

This is very good with haricot beans or braised celery to accompany the dish.

Lamb and mutton lend themselves particularly well to curried dishes. Here are one or two you may like to try, using left-overs of cold meat.

Mutton à l'Indienne

Slices of cold lamb or mutton
1 large onion
1 dessertsp. curry powder
2 oz butter

1 tab. chutney
1 tab. flour
¾ pint stock
Chopped parsley

Melt the butter, and slice the onion into it with a sprinkling of the parsley. Cook until light brown. Now add the curry powder, the chutney and the stock. Stir well and cook for a few minutes. Thicken this with the flour, add the slices of meat, and cook for a further 10–15 minutes or until thoroughly heated.

Serve with a border of rice or mashed potato.

Minced lamb, cooked with chopped onion and curry sauce made as in the above recipe, can be used to make these dishes: A few sultanas bring out the flavour of the curry.

Rissoles. Bind mince with beaten egg. Form into rissoles. Dip in egg and breadcrumb and fry in deep fat. Curry sauce can be served separately.

Pancakes. Have the mince piping hot ready to put into the centre of the cooked pancake. Roll up, and serve immediately. A green salad is good with this. The mince should be well flavoured with the curry for this recipe.

Lasagne. Lean minced lamb, well-curried, can be used instead of beef to make a variation of the recipe already given on page 66.

And curried mince, served with a border of curried, instead of plain, rice and a variety of vegetables in season, takes a lot of beating on a cold day.

Tomato Braede

This is a South African recipe. The dish is quite unlike our own stews, as it has not much gravy.

4 lean lamb cutlets or chops	Salt, pepper, basil
2 large onions	Cupful of stock or water
4 large tomatoes	Small new potatoes

Butter a deep stew-jar, and put a layer of tomatoes and onions at the bottom. Put in 2 cutlets, then another layer of tomatoes and onions, then the remaining 2 cutlets and the rest of the tomatoes. Sprinkle salt, pepper and a little finely chopped basil on each layer of tomatoes.

Add the cupful of stock or water. If the tomatoes are really juicy this may not be necessary.

Cover tightly, and stand in a slow to moderate oven for just over an hour. Remove from oven, add as many small new potatoes as required, add a very little stock if it seems too dry, replace lid, and cook for a further 1½ hours.

Chicken and Ham Patties

1 lb short crust pastry
8 oz minced cooked chicken
4 oz minced ham
1 tab. sweet chutney or pickle

4 tabs. of parsley or cheese sauce, or 1 small tin of asparagus or celery condensed soup
1 egg

Warm the sauce or soup and beat in most of the egg. Then add the minced meat, pickle and seasoning.

Roll out the pastry thinly and cut into 3-inch rounds for the bottom and 2½-inch rounds for the top of the patties. Line deep patty tins or deep bun tins with the 3-inch rounds, and fill with the chicken and ham mixture. Put on the lids, sealing the edges with a little of the beaten egg.

Prick the tops to allow steam to escape, and glaze with rest of the egg.

Bake in a hot oven for about 20 minutes.

Chicken Cottage Pie

1½ lb cold cooked chicken meat
2 rashers
2 small onions
1 oz butter

½ pint chicken stock
2 tabs. thin cream
1 egg
Mashed potato

Simmer chopped onion, and garlic if liked, in the butter for a few minutes.

Mince the chicken and rashers and mix with the onion. Moisten with chicken stock and cream and put into a greased pie dish.

Add a lid – not too thick – of creamy mashed potatoes to which a beaten egg has been added. Season with salt, pepper and a pinch of nutmeg, and spread on top of the mixture with a fork.

Cook for about 30 minutes in a fairly hot oven.

A purée of tomatoes, mushroom or cheese sauce, or a simple green salad all go well with this dish.

Chicken with Tarragon

    1 chicken
    1 bunch tarragon
    ¼ lb butter

Chop half the tarragon and blend with half the butter. Put the mixture inside the chicken, and the rest of the butter into a fireproof baking dish to melt.

Put in the bird, making sure that it is coated in the butter by turning it once or twice. The oven should be fairly hot for the first 20 minutes or so of cooking. Turn the bird fairly frequently. Lower heat after 30 minutes, and allow another 20–30 minutes for the bird to brown properly.

Serve decorated with sprigs of tarragon. Hot vegetables or a green salad go equally well with this dish.

Fricassee of Chicken

1 small cooked chicken
2 hard-boiled eggs
½ pint mixed milk and chicken stock
½ lb long-grained rice

Seasoning
1 oz butter
1 oz flour
2 tabs. cream

Make a white sauce with the melted butter, flour and milk and stock. Stir while it thickens, and then season with salt and pepper.

Cut the chicken into fairly thick pieces and heat very gently in this sauce.

Before serving, remove from heat and add cream and chopped egg whites. Serve on a bed of hot rice garnished with sliced egg yolks and sprinkled with paprika. This is a light, tasty and pretty dish.

Mock Goose

When you have been given yet another marrow in one week, try cooking it like this. The marrow should be a young one – not one of those Harvest Festival barrage balloons with a skin like teak – and the stuffing can be of any left-over meat of good quality.

Peel the marrow and cut it lengthwise at about a third of its depth. Scoop out any seeds. If really young, there should be very little waste. The deep part of the marrow will be stuffed; the shallower part will form the lid.

For the stuffing, mince about 1 lb of cold meat, not too fat, with 4 or 5 rashers. Put in appropriate herbs, such as sage with pork, oregano or basil with lamb, and seasoning of pepper and salt.

Stuff the cavity with this mixture, and dot with butter. Rub the marrow with flour, put on the marrow lid, and run a skewer through in several places (with a cruel stabbing action!) so that the juices of the cooking stuffing will flavour the marrow case.

Put it in a casserole, dotting well with butter. Put the lid on the casserole and bake slowly for an hour. It is a good idea to baste it several times. Remove the lid, and cook for a further half hour, basting rather more often.

This is very good with tomato sauce. Serve it in the casserole.

And here is another tasty marrow dish, using fresh minced beef.

Beef and Marrow Casserole

1 medium-sized marrow	2 oz Parmesan cheese
1 lb minced raw steak	3 oz breadcrumbs
1 small onion	3 tomatoes
1 tsp. chopped parsley	Seasoning
Beef dripping for frying	1 egg

Mince the meat, parsley, onion and seasoning. Melt a little good beef dripping and fry the meat mixture gently. Add grated cheese and beaten egg, and the breadcrumbs moistened with a little milk. Mix well together, with the seasoning.

Peel the marrow and remove seeds. Cut it into slices about 1 inch thick, and fry lightly in dripping.

Butter a casserole and fill it with alternating layers of the meat filling, sliced tomatoes and marrow.

Pour a cupful of tomato juice either fresh, from a tin, or made with diluted tomato purée, over all, cover closely and cook in a moderate oven for 1½–2 hours.

Sweets

Autumn is the time of the apple harvest, that useful crop which we rely on to carry us through the winter months, and longer, with luck.

In my garden there is a small apple tree, attractive in shape and very pretty with blossom in May. It bears medium-sized apples of bright red and yellow colouring. In theory, it is an eating apple. It tastes perfectly horrible and is rather hard.

Then I read, in one of Elizabeth David's cookery books, that French cooks often use a hard eating apple for their cooked apple dishes. I tried this recipe with my disappointing apples and they were transformed into something absolutely delicious.

Apples with Butter

Peel and slice the apples as usual. Add caster sugar and a generous knob of butter, and a squeeze of lemon juice, if liked. Cover and simmer until tender, and serve hot. You will probably not want cream with this dish, for the butter takes its place.

It is best, I find, to cook just enough to be eaten at the one meal, for buttered apples are not very appetizing when they are cold, although they would make an excellent filling for a plate-pie or similar pastry dish with the addition, perhaps, of cinnamon and sultanas, or any other flavouring that marries well with apple.

Banana and Black-currant Sweet

I first came across this attractive sweet, and the unusual blend of fruits, at Winchelsea, many years ago. The master of the house was the cook, and he told me that he had brought the recipe with him from South Africa.

For 4 people use:

> 4 bananas
> 3 tabs. black-currant jam or purée
> 1 pint custard (see Boiled Custard recipe)

Split the bananas lengthwise and arrange in a criss-cross fashion at the bottom of a bowl.

Spoon the jam over the bananas. It should be fairly runny. Thin it down with a little hot water if it is stiff.

Now pour over the custard and set the dish aside to cool.

A quick and easy sweet can be made by slicing a banana per person into individual dishes, adding a little black-currant purée or Ribena, and serving with plain yoghurt or thin cream.

Try whisking a small tin of black-currant purée with half a pint of plain yoghurt. It makes a beautiful clean-tasting dish. Most people prefer this without sugar, but put the sugar-sifter on the table for those who need it.

Bread and Butter Pudding with Pears

Here is a recipe from Anne Hughes' *Diary of a Farmer's Wife.*
She wrote out this recipe on August 25th, 1796.

'You doe peel sum pares, then putt sum peeses of bredde and
butter in thee bottom off a deep dyshe, and laye thee pares on
toppe, then more bredde and butter, throwing on sum sugger
ande a pinsh of cynamon. Then you doe take 4 eggs ande beate
them harde for a bitte the putt them in a messure of mylke ande
beete uppe till frothie, then poore over thee puddinge in thee
dyshe and cooke itt gentlie for a hower bye thee clocke.'

Some months later she gives a fascinating recipe for 'A Violet
Pudden' with the comment: 'It beeing a good cure for cross
husbands,' but as it needs 6 handfuls of dried violets, for a start,
I think it impractical to include it.

Pears in Red Wine

This is a dish which always pleases. The pears emerge a beautiful
mahogany brown, complete with stalks, and with the most
superb flavour.

Simply peel as many pears, but leave on the stalks, as you will need, and put them in a deep casserole with a liquor made of half red wine and water. This should almost cover them.

Now add 6–8 oz of vanilla sugar according to the amount of liquid being used – 8 oz should be ample for a pint of mixed wine and water – and cook in a slow oven for 3 hours. Some pears may need longer cooking still before turning the deep red which is so attractive.

Serve in their own syrup, with cream, either hot or cold.

Apple Amber

2 lb cooking apples
4 oz sugar
3 oz butter

Rind and juice of 1 lemon
3 eggs
1 tab. caster sugar for each egg white

Put sugar, butter, juice and grated rind of lemon into a saucepan with the peeled and sliced apples. Simmer until tender, then beat to a purée with a fork or in the blender.

Beat up the 3 yolks of eggs and add to the mixture. Put into a deep greased fireproof dish, and cook in a very gentle oven for 20–30 minutes.

Whip the whites stiffly, fold in the castor sugar, and put the meringue on top. The pudding will need a further 10 minutes or so to brown this nicely.

The butter, egg yolks and gentle cooking all combine to give the apples the lovely golden colour which gives the dish its name.

Apple Charlotte

Here is an old-fashioned pudding which most men enjoy. It goes down well on a cold day and is reasonably substantial.

For 4 people you will need:

2 lb cooking apples
5 oz sugar

A spoonful or two of water

Several slices of thin white bread and butter

Grease a round soufflé dish and line it with the finely-cut white buttered bread. Be lavish with the butter!

Peel and core the apples. Slice them finely and put a layer of apples, then sugar, then bread and butter, repeating the process until the dish is full. Finish with a layer of bread and butter.

Cover with greased paper and bake in a slowish oven for 45 minutes. Sprinkle well with sugar before bringing to the table.

This should really turn out successfully, but if you are too timid to risk it then serve it in the dish in which it was cooked. It will taste just as good.

Apple Snow

This is very quick and simple to prepare, and deliciously light.

2 lb cooking apples (Bramleys are best)

5 oz caster sugar

2 egg whites

Simmer the sliced and peeled apples with the sugar and just enough water to prevent burning. When thoroughly tender, beat until fluffy with a fork.

Whisk egg whites stiffly, and when the apples are cool, fold in the egg whites until you have a light fluffy mixture.

Pile it into an attractive bowl and chill before serving with cream.

Chocolate Mousse and Variations

Nothing is simpler to make than the well-tried and popular chocolate mousse. All that is needed for 4 generous helpings is:

4 oz bitter chocolate and 4 eggs

Melt the chocolate, and beat in the yolks of the eggs. Whip up the 4 whites stiffly and fold into the mixture.

The juice of an orange, added to the chocolate and yolks mixture *before* the addition of the whites, makes an interesting variation of this dish; or a dessertspoon of Aurum, Cointreau or any other orange liqueur is equally good.

Some people like a dessertspoon of brandy in place of the orange liquid.

Always serve chocolate mousse in small dishes. It is very filling.

Bread and Butter Pudding

A well-made bread and butter pudding can be delicious. This serves 4–6 people.

6 thin slices white bread	2 oz caster sugar
2 oz butter	2 eggs
3 oz mixed sultanas, currants, seedless raisins	1 pint milk

Butter bread, remove crusts and cut into neat fingers. Line a greased pie-dish with some of them.

Sprinkle in half the fruit and put another layer of bread and butter.

Beat eggs well with the milk and sugar Pour almost all into the dish.

Put on the final layer of bread and butter fingers, this time *butter side up.* Add the rest of the egg, milk and sugar mixture.

Bake fairly slowly, so that the bread absorbs the liquid well, in a slow oven for about an hour.

Orange Pudding

This is an unusual pudding and useful because the ingredients are always to hand. It is light enough for invalids to enjoy and a little different from the insipid milk puddings which are so often their lot.

For 4 people you will need:

2 oranges   ¾ pint milk
3 oz caster sugar   1 tab. cornflour
2 eggs

Wash the oranges and peel them finely. Remove pith.

Put the rind with the milk and sugar into a saucepan and warm slowly, so that the liquid is well infused.

Mix cornflour with a little milk in a basin, and when the hot milk boils, pour it through a strainer into the cornflour mixture and then return to the pan, stirring until the sauce thickens.

Slice the oranges and place in a fireproof greased dish. Separate whites from yolks of eggs, keeping the whites for the meringue top.

Beat the yolks and add them to the orange-flavoured sauce. Pour over the oranges, and put dish in a warm place.

Whisk whites, fold in a dessertspoon of sugar and arrange on top. Brown in a slow oven for about 10–15 minutes.

Charlotte Marsala

This is one of the few really rich sweets given in this book. A little goes a long way.

8 oz sponge fingers   5 egg yolks
5 oz butter   ¼ pint cream for masking
5 oz icing sugar   Wineglass Marsala or Dram-
5 oz chopped walnuts   buie
                     Walnut halves for decoration

Well grease a 6-inch loose-bottomed cake tin. Split sponge fingers and trim them to the same length, just a little longer than the depth of the cake tin.

Dip them quickly in the Marsala and line the tin.

Now mix all the other ingredients, except cream and walnut halves, together to a stiffish paste and put carefully into the centre of the tin. Spread evenly, and put into the refrigerator to set.

Before serving, push out of the tin, mask with the whipped cream and decorate with a few halved walnuts.

A Few Autumn Preserves

Japonica Jelly

I must stress that not all japonica fruits make good jelly. The one which grows on the front of my house is known variously as Cydonia Japonica, Japanese Quince and Chaenomeles Lagenaria. It is the common vivid-red variety, and produces quite large green 'apples' which start to fall in early October. They are too hard to chop with a knife and I simply wash them, put them with cold water in my largest saucepan and let them simmer until tender, when I attempt this annual recipe.

The jelly is bright red in colour, rather tart, excellent as an accompaniment to lamb or game, as well as having its more obvious use as a tea-time preserve.

Cover the washed fruit with cold water and simmer until really tender. Strain through a jelly bag overnight.

Allow one pound of preserving sugar to each pint of liquid, and boil, skimming frequently, until the jelly sets on a cold plate.

Crab Apple Jelly

This is made in exactly the same way, and usually about the same time of year. It is one of the last preserves to make, and I always find it enormously satisfying to bring home a basketful of these little wild apples which have cost me nothing except an enjoyable walk and some health-giving bending.

The delicious scent of crab apples simmering is a wonderful autumnal pleasure in itself.

I try to pot all jellies in small half-pound jars, if possible. Once opened, jelly seems to deteriorate more quickly than jam, I find.

Quince Jam

Here is another late preserve of the Autumn. It becomes more and more difficult to procure these golden pear-shaped fruits with their ancient and unforgettable scent. Sometimes the local Women's Institute stall in the market can supply them in late September or early October, and some old gardens still have a flourishing tree.

The jam has an earthy fruitiness quite unlike any other preserve, and the colour is a rich ruby-red.

I make Quince Jam like this:

Peel, core and slice 8 to 10 quinces. Cover with cold water to which the juice of a lemon has been added. Cook gently until the fruit is soft.

Add 2-3 lb of preserving sugar, boil rapidly, stirring frequently, until the jam sets on a plate.

These quantities will make about 5 or 6 lb of jam.

Marrow and Ginger Jam

5½ lb marrow
5½ lb preserving sugar
3 lemons
½ lb crystallized ginger
¾ cupful salt

Skin, de-seed and chop up the marrow into little cubes. Weigh out 5½ lb. Sprinkle with the salt and forget it for 12 hours.

Now *strain well*. Sprinkle on all the sugar and put aside for a further 12 hours.

Finely peel the lemons and put the rind and juice into a large saucepan with the marrow, sugar and chopped ginger. Boil altogether until the marrow is golden and translucent and the jam sets on a cold plate.

Bramble Jelly

Despite wrecked stockings, stained fingers and scratched arms everyone enjoys blackberry picking. There are plenty of recipes for blackberry and apple jam, but I prefer to make jelly and here give the recipe I use. Remember that blackberries alone lack the amount of pectin which the apples lend them, so that the lemon juice is absolutely necessary for a successful set. A few unripe blackberries – not *green*, of course, but red and hard – among the black beauties, help to set the jelly.

> 4 lb blackberries
> Juice of 2 lemons
> ¾ pint water
> 1 lb of preserving sugar to
> each strained pint of liquid

Simmer washed blackberries with water and lemon juice until tender. This will take about 30 minutes. Squash them well with a fork, pour into a jelly bag and strain overnight.

Now return to pan allowing 1 lb of sugar to each pint of liquid. Let sugar dissolve slowly, then boil rapidly, skimming frequently, until the jelly sets on a plate. This should happen in about 10 minutes, but may take a little longer depending on the ripeness of the berries.

Pour into warmed jars and look forward to eating it.

These quantities should yield about 3–4 lb of ruby-red jelly.

General Guide to making Mixed Pickles

Surplus vegetables can easily be turned into tasty pickles. Shallots, small onions, beetroot, cauliflower, cucumbers, walnuts and mushrooms are just a few which come to mind.

Cut the available ingredients into neat small pieces – onions, shallots and beetroot, of course, will need to be peeled and the last will need to be cooked first. Put them into a china bowl, sprinkle well with salt and leave for 24 hours.

Drain well and pack into clean jars. Cover with spiced vinegar either HOT or COLD according to the recipe, and use after 4–6 weeks storage.

Spiced vinegar is made thus:

> 4 pints *top quality* malt vinegar
> ¼ lb mixed pickling spice
> 1 dessertsp. salt
> 1 onion

Put the vinegar into an enamel or aluminium pan. Other metal pans are unsuitable.

Tie the spices together in a muslin bag and put in the vinegar with salt and chopped onion. Simmer for 10 minutes and strain.

When cold it can be used for pickling cabbage, cauliflower, onions and other vegetables. Use it hot for such things as walnuts and plums, but consult the individual recipe when about to pickle.

Green Tomato Chutney

The moment of bitter truth comes to all outdoor tomato growers just before the frosts arrive. There they stand, those cherished tomato plants, with more green tomatoes upon them than the red ones which have already been eaten.

Make the best of a bad job. Pick the poor things and turn them into chutney. Here is a country recipe:

3 lb green tomatoes	1 lb Demerara sugar
4 cooking apples	1 dessertsp. ground ginger
1 cucumber	1 dessertsp. mustard
4 onions	½ tsp. cayenne pepper
4 oz sultanas	1 quart vinegar

Peel and slice apples, onions and cucumber. Chop tomatoes.

Put all the ingredients together in a large pan and bring gently to the boil. Simmer for about an hour or longer, until the mixture is thoroughly soft, stirring frequently.

Put into warm jars and seal.

And here is a simple sweet chutney which can be made at any time:

Sweet Chutney

1 lb dates	1 tab. ground ginger
3 lb cooking apples	½ tsp. cayenne pepper
1 lb onions	1 tab. allspice
	1 quart vinegar

Peel, and chop apples and onions. Chop up the dates, and put all the ingredients into a large pan. Boil for about an hour, and bottle when cold.

Winter

Charles Kingsley's glad cry of 'Welcome, wild north-easter!' gets no echoing support from me. If I had lashings of money and no ties I would set off for a sunny spot after Christmas and come back at the beginning of April in time for the primroses.

I suspect that the reverend poet wrote that by a roaring fire with toasted crumpets on the fender and a steaming pot of tea to hand. For there is no doubt about it, the pleasures of the tea-table really come into their own at Winter-time.

Now is the time to relish that home-made strawberry jam which we stirred on a sweltering June afternoon. And now is the time, too, to make thick soups, luscious with leeks and onions, to ease our winter colds. Savoury casserole dishes, pork pies, pigeon pics, pilaffs and hot-pots, all fragrant and warming, are the dishes to keep out the wild north-easter and all the other bleak horrors of Winter.

Yes, Winter cooking can be very rewarding. Besides, the kitchen is usually the warmest room in the house!

Soups

Scotch Broth

1 lb neck of mutton	1 turnip
1 onion	2 oz pearl barley
1 carrot	1 tab. chopped parsley
1 leek	3 pints stock
2 sticks of celery	

Cut meat from bones, removing any fat. Put meat, bones and stock into a large stewpan. Bring to the boil and skim thoroughly. Wash and blanch the barley. Add it to the mixture, seasoning at the same time. Simmer for an hour. Add all the vegetables, diced, and simmer for a further hour.

Remove bones, skim fat, add the chopped parsley and serve.

To blanch either rice or barley, wash first, then cover with cold water, bring to the boil, strain and rinse in cold water.

Minestrone

There is no hard-and-fast rule for the recipe for this popular thick soup but here is a reliable one which can be adapted by any resourceful cook with similar ingredients available. Herbs, vegetables, any kind of small pasta, good stock and grated cheese are the basic necessities.

2 tomatoes
3 carrots
3 leeks
1 large onion
1 turnip
1 celery stick
1 large potato
2 oz vermicelli or spaghetti

Chopped herbs, parsley, thyme and basil. (Some recipes include sage, but go easily with this if you are cooking for people whose tastes you don't know)
2 pints stock
Parmesan cheese

Dice vegetables, but not the potato. Chop celery very finely. Simmer all in 1 tab. of olive oil at the bottom of the stewpan with the herbs. When golden brown, add the stock, the diced potato, and vermicelli and simmer for 20–30 minutes.

Dried beans are another useful ingredient, but must be soaked overnight if included.

Serve with generous quantity of grated Parmesan cheese.

Beef Tea

1 lb lean beef (shin is good)
1 pint water
Pinch of salt

Mince beef finely and put it into a tall casserole. Cover with water and add salt. Let it stand for an hour, stirring it now and again to release juices. Put on the lid. Place casserole in a saucepan of cold water. The water should be about two-thirds up the casserole, cover, and simmer for 2–3 hours. Alternatively, place casserole in a pan of water in the oven, for the same length of time.

Strain the beef tea through a coarse strainer or sieve. Too fine a strainer will keep back nourishing particles. Remove any specks of fat with soft paper.

A little sherry or Madeira can turn this into an excellent clear soup.

White Winter Soup

This is a cheap and particularly warming soup, very comforting to sufferers with colds. The ingredients are almost always to hand throughout the winter months and it is quick and easy to prepare.

2 sticks celery
2 leeks
2 onions

1½ pints white stock or water
½ pint milk
1 oz butter

Melt the butter and add chopped vegetables. Cook gently for 10 minutes, stirring occasionally to prevent sticking. Pour on stock, season, and simmer till vegetables are soft. Pass through a sieve, return to the saucepan and add milk. Reheat, and serve with croûtons or chopped chives or parsley.

Tomato Soup (1)

1½ lb tomatoes or tin of Italian variety
1 onion
2 oz butter
1 rasher

1 bay leaf
4 sugar lumps
2 pints stock
¼ pint thin cream
Pepper and salt

Slice skinned tomatoes and onion into melted butter in the stewpan. Add chopped rasher, bay leaf and sugar. Simmer to-

gether until tender. Add stock and seasoning, and simmer for
20–30 minutes.

Remove bay leaf. Put mixture through sieve or mill and then
return it to the pan. Heat almost to boiling point, add cream
and serve with croûtons.

Tomato Soup (2)

Lighter than 1st recipe

> 1½ lb tomatoes or 1 tin of Italian
> skinned tomatoes
> 2 tabs. small sago or tapioca
> 2 pints stock
> Pepper and salt

Stew tomatoes in their own juice and put through sieve or
fine mill. Add stock. Boil and thicken with the sago or tapioca.
Season, simmer for 20 minutes, and serve sprinkled with a pinch
of chopped parsley on top.

Lentil Soup

The stock which is left after simmering salt beef or pork lends
itself well to this nourishing soup, but be sure that it is not *too*
salt. If so, use half stock and half water.

> ½ lb red lentils
> 1 large onion
> 1 oz butter
> 2 pints of stock

Wash lentils and slice onion. Melt butter and let onion cook
for 5 minutes in it. Add lentils and stock. Bring to boiling point
and remove scum. Simmer gently for 1½ hours at least. Sieve,
reheat, and serve sprinkled with chopped parsley.

Curry Soup

This somewhat neglected soup is particularly good on a cold winter's night.

> 1 dessertsp. curry powder
> 3 oz Patna rice
> 2 pints brown or white stock

Mix curry powder to a paste with a little of the stock. Heat the remainder of the stock until it boils. Pour on to curry paste, then return all to saucepan, stirring the while. When it is boiling, add rice, and allow to simmer for about 30 minutes.

Chopped watercress makes a good garnish.

Vermicelli Soup

This attractive white soup is quickly made and is useful when vegetarians are among your guests.

> 1½ oz vermicelli
> 1 oz grated cheese
> 2 pints white stock
> Seasoning

Bring stock to boiling point. Drop in vermicelli and simmer for 15 minutes. Just before serving, add grated cheese. Stir well, and serve with croûtons.

Hors d'oeuvre

Winter Salads and Cooked Vegetables

These can be used as part of a mixed hors d'oeuvre, supplying 'the raw' and 'the gentle and smooth' ingredients.

Cole Slaw

Use the inner leaves of white cabbage. Slice finely and blend with some thinnish mayonnaise.

Red Cabbage

Shred as for cole slaw, but cover with salt and leave for 48 hours. Drain well, cover with spiced vinegar and allow it to marinade for a further 48 hours.

Potato Salad

If you can get hold of some new potatoes in this bleak season your potato salad will be improved. If not, Majestic are about the most satisfactory winter one for this recipe.

Cook, cut into dice when cold, and mix with some finely chopped onion or shallot. Mix with thinnish mayonnaise.

Leek Vinaigrette

Use only the white part of the leek. Cut into equal lengths. Cook for 10-15 minutes in salted water. Drain, and dress with vinaigrette sauce (2 of oil to 1 of vinegar). Chopped chives or parsley garnishes this well.

Cauliflower Vinaigrette is a similar dish, treated as the one above. Break the cauliflower into neat small pieces before boiling, and don't cook it too long, or your pretty pieces will turn to mush.

Beetroot diced, or sliced, is a marvellous standby for a mixed hors d'oeuvre and any of the frozen or tinned vegetables which you will find mentioned more lengthily in their fresh conditions under the Summer hors d'oeuvre section, e.g. young carrots, peas, beans, etc., are a great help in providing colour and blandness to the mixed hors d'oeuvre. Tinned sweet corn makes a cheerful addition to a winter hors d'oeuvre.

Ham and Pineapple Circles

Brown bread and butter
Thinly sliced ham
Pineapple rings
Cream cheese
Garnish

Cut the buttered bread and the ham into a circle the same size as the pineapple ring. Make sure that the ham is lean and the pineapple well-drained.

Put the ham on the brown bread, the pineapple on the ham and spread lightly with cream cheese. An olive can be set in the middle, or a slice of tomato, or sprig of watercress, or even a sprinkling of paprika alone.

Rollmop Herrings

Someone once said – a Scotsman probably – that herrings and oatmeal could be considered a perfectly balanced diet. Herrings certainly abound in protein, and the advantage of the following recipe is that the finished product will keep safely for at least three weeks and provide several servings. That is why I have allowed double quantities this time.

8 herrings	2 bay leaves
2 finely chopped shallots or	½ pint malt vinegar
1 small onion	1 pint water
4 small gherkins	2 oz salt

Clean fish and remove back bones. Cut off heads, and if the herrings are large, cut them into neat fillets. Put salt into the pint of water, and soak fish in this brine for about 3 hours.

Take them from the brine and immerse them in vinegar for about the same time. Remove, and roll each fish or fillet round the chopped shallot.

Pack into jars with bay leaves and gherkins and pour over cold spiced vinegar.

This is made by boiling a tablespoon of pickling spices with a pint of vinegar for 10 minutes. Strain before covering the fish.

Rollmops look attractive served with sliced red and green peppers, or lettuce, of course.

Pork Liver Pâté

1 lb pig's liver	3 tabs. stock
½ lb belly of pork	2 tabs. sherry or white wine
2 eggs	Pinch of mace
¼ pint cream	Salt and pepper

Put liver and belly of pork through fine mincer *twice*. Blend with the rest of the ingredients to a smooth paste, then pack into a greased 1-lb loaf tin.

Stand the tin in a bain-marie, or baking tin half full of water, and cook in a slow oven for about 1½ hours. The pâté will begin to come away from the sides of the dish when it is cooked through.

Leave it to cool in the tin. It is a good idea to place a weight on top as it cools, as the pâté will slice more neatly if the texture is firm.

Serve cut in slices with hot toast. Lemon wedges and crisp lettuce make a good garnish.

Chicken Liver Pâté

1 lb chicken livers	½ clove garlic
2 oz butter	2 tabs. brandy
1 shallot	

Simmer finely chopped garlic and shallot in the butter until soft.

Add the cleaned livers to the pan. Stir occasionally whilst cooking. This should take about 5–7 minutes. Mash finely, add brandy, beat together, and then transfer to a sieve.

When sieved put the mixture into your greased terrine or loaf tin, smooth the top and stand it in the bain-marie as for Pork Liver Pâté.

This pâté will cook in about half an hour, as the ingredients have been partly cooked already. Chill well before serving, sliced, with hot toast.

Goose liver also makes excellent pâté.

Salami and Bean Salad

½ lb shelled cooked broad beans or 8-oz packet of frozen broad or lima beans
¼ lb salami or well-flavoured continental sausage, in the piece

1 small onion
1 lettuce
Vinaigrette sauce

Chop onion finely and mix with cold cooked beans. Skin the sausage, dice it, and mix with other ingredients. Toss in the vinaigrette sauce and arrange on bed of crisped lettuce. Serve at once.

White haricot beans can be used for this dish. Soak them overnight, and simmer until they are just cooked – if possible in a weakish ham stock. Cool and use as above.

Cod's Roe Pâté (Cooked)

1 lb smoked cod's roe
2 oz butter
1 tab. cream
1 clove of garlic or garlic salt
Black pepper

Skin the roe and put into a bowl. Add butter, garlic and pepper, and mix until smooth. Gradually add the cream, and blend well.

Stand the bowl in a bain-marie and cook slowly for 20–30 minutes in a fairly slow oven. Cover top with foil to keep the pâté moist.

Lettuce, tomato, or watercress all make good garnishes. Hot toast should be served with it.

Here is another *uncooked* version:

1 lb smoked cod's roe
3 tabs. white breadcrumbs
¼ pint cream

4 tabs. lemon juice
3 tabs. chopped chives or parsley
Black pepper

Pound the skinned roe to a paste, and blend in soft breadcrumbs and cream.

Now add chopped herbs, lemon juice and pepper to taste. Chill well, and serve sliced with lettuce, lemon wedges, and hot toast.

Curried Consommé

¾ pint cold consommé or 1 medium tin
4–6 oz mild cream cheese
1 tsp. curry powder

Whisk the ingredients together. Put into small individual dishes. Chill well. Garnish with chopped parsley, chives or a pinch of paprika.

Macaroni Cheese

Remember that macaroni, vermicelli, spaghetti and other pastas must be cleaned first by dropping them into fast-boiling water for about 3 minutes. *Never cold water.* After draining, transfer them to the vessel in which they will be cooked.

> 3 oz macaroni
> ½–¾ pint Béchamel sauce
> 4 oz grated cheese (Parmesan or Cheddar)
> Pepper, salt, and a little grated nutmeg

Break the macaroni into short lengths and cook in plenty of salted water for about 20 minutes. Strain and put into a buttered fireproof dish or individual dishes. Sprinkle three quarters of the grated cheese among the macaroni, season carefully. Pour over the Béchamel sauce, and cover the top with the rest of the grated cheese. Cook in a fairly brisk oven, until lightly browned, for about 25 minutes.

Macaroni blends well with the following mixture:

> 1 clove garlic
> 1 shallot
> 4 olives
> 2 or 3 anchovies

Mince all together, and cook gently in a spoonful of olive oil. Stir the resultant brew into the cooked macaroni. Put into fireproof dish, as before, and allow 20 minutes to heat thoroughly.

Or try it à l'Italienne:

Fry a shredded onion in a little melted butter, and when it is cooked stir in about 6 tabs. of cooked macaroni with 2 tabs. of grated Gruyère or Parmesan cheese. Serve very hot in individual dishes garnished with strips of anchovy.

Beef Marrow on Toast

Our forebears were very fond of marrow, but for some reason – possibly because it is fattening – it has gone out of favour. Try it, one cold night, for a change.

Butter some squares of hot toast and spread with the hot marrow, sprinkled with salt and cayenne or black pepper.

The marrow, removed from the bone of course, should be simmered in a little salted water for about 5 minutes. Drain well before spreading.

Winter is the time for making use of onions. They can provide an attractive first course if served in one of the following ways:

Onion Purée

Make a thick purée of cooked onions and serve surrounded by cooked spaghetti, vermicelli or fluffy mashed potato. A creamy white or cheese sauce, sprinkled with chopped chives, parsley, or paprika, tops the dish. Serve very hot.

Stuffed Onions

The large mild Spanish onion is really better than our own stronger variety for this dish, but if you are an onion-lover then the British will suit you very well.

Simmer the peeled onions, being careful to keep their shape. Lift from saucepan and put in greased fireproof dish, first removing a little of the central core of each onion. Mix this with a stuffing of finely chopped ham, or cooked mushroom, chicken or veal well-seasoned. Stuff each onion. Put a piece of butter on top, braise for about 20–30 minutes, and serve hot.

Onions with Cheese Sauce

Boil onions, drain, and break into pieces. Put in a fireproof dish
and cover with good cheese sauce. Put small pieces of butter on
top and sprinkle with breadcrumbs. Cook in moderate oven
for about 20 minutes.

Onion Pancakes

Make ½ pint batter with 3 oz flour, 1 egg, and ½ pint milk, and
grate 1 large onion into this mixture. Fry a pancake for each
person to be served and keep warm.

Stuff each with a filling of minced ham and chopped egg.
Roll up each pancake and place neatly in a fireproof dish. Cover
with cheese sauce. It will need only 10–15 minutes in the oven.

This is very filling, and could be used as a vegetarian dish –
omitting ham and substituting minced vegetables – for a main
course.

Onions, chopped finely with a little parsley, make an excellent
flavouring for an omelette. Add them to the beaten eggs before
cooking.

Main Dishes

Cod is at its best in the Winter months, although it can be bought at any time of the year. It can be cooked in many ways, although I don't think that the cooks at a school which I once attended, were aware of the fact.

On Fridays we filed into the dining hall to face the truly gruesome sight of a whole boiled cod curled unnaturally upon a thick white dish. Its poor parboiled eyes protruded like hat-pin knobs, and it lay there, slimy and grey, in a fast-congealing puddle of fishy water.

Accompanied by boiled potatoes *au naturel*, complete with grey patches and plenty of eyes, this was one of the dreariest and most revolting meals I can remember. If I remember aright, we were also obliged to speak in French only on that day. What with one thing and another, conversation languished. It takes a lot to quell schoolgirls' ebullience, but boiled cod is enough to dampen anyone's spirits.

Here are a few more sprightly methods of presenting cod. It is rather coarse-grained, like haddock, whose living areas it shares in the northern waters around our island. These recipes will be found equally suitable for fresh haddock.

Cod with Hollandaise Sauce

2½ lb cod in the piece
2 oz butter
1 tab. flour

2 egg yolks
Juice of 1 lemon
Pepper and salt

Simmer cod in salted water for about 20 minutes. Drain well, and put it on a hot dish garnished with parsley.

Serve at once with the Hollandaise sauce, made as follows:

Melt the butter, add flour, stirring well, then add gradually a cupful of the fish liquor in which the cod has been cooked. Stir until the sauce is smooth.

Beat the 2 egg yolks and put them in the sauce-boat which will be carried to the table. Add the lemon juice, beat again. Pour the sauce over the egg and lemon mixture, stir briskly, season with salt and pepper, and the sauce is then ready.

Cod Lyonnaise

1½ lb cod
1½ lb potatoes
2 onions
¼ lb bacon

2 oz butter
¼ lb grated cheese
½ lb peeled cooked tomatoes
or a small tin
Pepper, salt and basil, if liked

Slice the peeled potatoes and put a layer in the bottom of a casserole. Cut the cod into small pieces, and put a layer on top of the potatoes.

Now slice the onion and cut the bacon into neat pieces. Arrange a layer on top of the cod. Dot with a little butter.

Continue forming these layers, until the ingredients are used up. The top layer should be of fish. Pour the cooked tomatoes over the mixture and dot with butter. Season to taste.

Cover and bake in a moderate oven for 40–50 minutes.

A Proper Fish Pie

The term 'fish pie' usually invokes a feeling of gloom. It takes us back to grisly school dinners or some appalling concoction created in war-time from one of the few misshapen and unknown objects on display at the fishmonger's. I still remember, with shuddering, a fearsome dead creature, pitch-black, with whiskers, and an expression like Boris Karloff's at his least benign, dominating the marble slab in the High Street at Witney about 1943.

I suppose somebody bought and ate it, probably in a fish pie. Cross my heart, this recipe isn't a bit like that.

1 lb cooked white fish
4 oz cooked salmon or 1 small tin
2 oz frozen prawns or shrimps (unfreeze before cooking)

½ pint well-flavoured white sauce – parsley or cheese
Mashed potatoes to which an egg has been added

Grease a shallow dish, flake the fish and mix in the prawns or shrimps. A sprinkling of tarragon can be added at this stage.

Cover with the sauce, parsley or cheese – or a spoonful of anchovy essence added to your white sauce instead would be equally nice – stir together, then add the lid of mashed potatoes, not too thick, and bake in a moderate oven for about half an hour.

If you do not want to use potatoes, simply sprinkle grated cheese on top of the fish and sauce mixture and cook as stated.

Stuffed Baked Herrings

Herrings are such wonderful value for money that it is a pity they are not more adventurously cooked. Here is a sustaining, cheap and easily digested meal for a cold day.

One herring for each person.

For stuffing: Sieved potatoes, nutmeg, salt, pepper and herbs to taste. Basil, fennel or parsley will all prove suitable additions for flavouring this stuffing.

Bone the herrings and flatten them.

The potato purée, flavoured with a pinch of nutmeg, and other seasonings, should now be spread thickly on one inner half of the herring. Fold to its normal shape, and wrap each stuffed fish in buttered foil. Place them in a shallow baking tin and cook in a moderate oven for 30–40 minutes.

Smoked Haddock and Sweet Corn

Smoked fillet of cod can be used, if preferred. You will need for 4 people:

1½ lb smoked haddock   1 oz butter
1 lb tin sweet corn   Seasoning

For white sauce

1 oz butter   ½ pint milk
1 oz flour   Salt and pepper

Put a generous layer of drained corn into a casserole. Cut
fish into squares or strips and arrange on the bed of corn, dotting
with a little butter, and sprinkling lightly with salt and pepper.
Put the rest of the corn over the fish.

Make ½ pint of white sauce and pour over the ingredients of
the casserole. Cover and cook gently for 30–40 minutes in a
moderate oven.

Remove lid about 5–10 minutes before serving so that the top
browns a little.

Spinach or puréed tomatoes go well with this dish, and if a
more substantial meal is needed then poached eggs, or *oeufs
mollet* can be served with it.

Oeufs mollet are eggs boiled to exactly the right degree, i.e.
with the white set but the yolk 'still dribbly' (as my sister used to
complain in her youth!). Shell them, and keep them warm, if
need be, in a basin of warm water before bringing them, as
speedily as possible, to the table.

Scallops

Scallops are in season during the winter months. They make an
attractive first course, but are quite substantial enough to form
the main dish for lunch.

The fishmonger usually sells them already opened and cleaned,
but if yours are not opened warm them in the oven and then use
the point of a knife to part the shells. Wash well, removing the
beard, and use the white and coral portions for cooking.

The simplest method of all is to simmer them in boiling salted water, acidulated with a tablespoonful of lemon juice or wine vinegar for 20 minutes.

More exciting recipes are as follows:

Scallops with Bacon

8 scallops
8 rashers
1 oz butter
Flour, salt and pepper

Cook the rashers gently until done. Remove to a hot dish and put the butter in the frying-pan with the bacon fat.

Dredge scallops in seasoned flour, put into the hot butter, and cook gently.

Add to the bacon and serve with a garnish of watercress or lemon wedges.

Poached Scallops

Poach as in the first recipe given, but make a good white sauce, Mornay or Velouté.

Chop the cooked scallops and mix with the sauce. Fill the shells, and serve with hot mashed potato piped round the edge.

Scallops en Brochette

8 small scallops
8 rashers
16 button mushrooms
Lemon juice
Butter
Pepper and salt

Squeeze lemon juice over the scallops, and dust with a little pepper. Wrap each in a rasher, and secure with wooden cocktail stick.

Put the rolls on a grill pan with the button mushrooms. Dot with a little butter. All will need to be turned about halfway through cooking time which should be about 10 minutes.

Serve with hot rice or a green salad dressed with French dressing or both. Some people prefer hot toast and butter with this dish instead.

The addition of curry powder at the seasoning stage turns this dish into *Scallops Indienne*. If you try this variation of the recipe then rice, of course, is the accompaniment, with a variety of chutneys.

Country cooks, in particular, deplore the dearth of rabbits. They supplied cheap, clean meat, easily digested and adaptable for a host of recipes. Thanks to myxamatosis, this source of meat is still looked upon with some suspicion.

Nevertheless, rabbit from overseas can be bought and those reared domestically (if they haven't been your own adored pets, of course) make excellent eating.

In the practically meatless days of war-time, I was once invited to supper by a charming Frenchwoman. She had prepared a delicious rabbit fricassee accompanied by a dish of buttered carrots ('so good for night-blindness') sprinkled with parsley. I remember her – and the fricassee – with deep affection.

Chicken, now rather cheaper, and certainly easier to obtain, will prove equally suitable for this recipe.

Rabbit Fricassee

1 young rabbit	2 oz chopped mushrooms
1 pint of milk and water, or milk and white stock	1 oz butter
	1 oz flour
4 oz chopped bacon	1 tsp. chopped parsley
1 large onion	Salt and pepper

Joint the rabbit and put into a large saucepan. Pour in mixed stock and milk and add the chopped onion, bacon, mushrooms and herbs. Season to taste.

Simmer gently for about 1½ hours or until the joints are tender. Lift them out and keep warm on a dish.

Strain the liquor. Melt the butter in a clean saucepan, stir in flour and make a good white sauce using the liquor. Pour over the rabbit joints and serve garnished with lemon wedges, parsley sprigs or watercress.

Any brightly coloured vegetable goes well with this pale dish. Those buttered carrots, for instance, of blessed memory, puréed tomatoes, spinach or sweet corn.

Pupton

This useful dish is an old English one, and chicken and turkey, duck and veal can all be used. I came across this interesting knowledge in an attractive cookery book called *Country Fare* by Mary Aylett, published some years ago.

The recipe she gives is for young pigeons, and here, in general terms is the method used.

Make a forcemeat of ¼ lb fat bacon or ham, ¼ lb chopped suet and a little chopped herbs, predominately parsley, and shallot. Mince all together and blend with about ½ lb soft white breadcrumbs, salt, pepper, nutmeg and grated lemon rind. Moisten with stock, and bind the forcemeat together with a well-beaten egg.

Clean and truss the pigeons. Put a layer of forcemeat in a deep fireproof dish and place the pigeons upon it. Fill the spaces with choice vegetables which will stand up to fairly long cooking – e.g. asparagus, mushrooms, young carrots, etc. Hard-boiled eggs make a tasty addition and also the pigeons' livers. Moisten with a little stock. Cover with the rest of the forcemeat, place greaseproof paper over the top, and cook for about an hour in a slow oven. Take off the paper for the last 10 minutes or so to brown the top.

This is equally good hot or cold.

Jugged hare is probably the best-known and best-liked way of cooking hare, and I shall not repeat the recipe which is so easily available.

If you can stand the sight of a hare dished up whole (which I can't) here is a recipe which was much liked, so it is said, by King Edward VII.

Hare à la Royale

1 medium-sized hare
¼ lb fat bacon
3 cloves of garlic
3 onions
2 carrots
Stock
1 egg

1 tab. chopped parsley
6 streaky rashers
2 tabs. flour
Glass of white or red wine
Salt and pepper
4 tabs. white breadcrumbs

Put aside the liver and blood. Make forcemeat by mincing the garlic, fat bacon, liver and parsley together with the white breadcrumbs. Bind altogether with well-beaten egg and season.

Stuff the hare with this mixture and sew the opening with fine string. Spread the rashers in an earthenware fireproof dish and curl the hare round on top. In centre, put the whole onions and sliced carrots. Add salt, pepper and put in the oven moistened with a little stock, and half the glass of white wine.

Now make the sauce by melting a little butter, thickening it with flour, and gradually adding the blood, the rest of the white wine, and more stock if needed. If you are feeling extravagant a dessertspoonful of brandy can now be added.

Pour this sauce over the hare, cover and cook gently for about 2½–3 hours. Serve with its sauce and rashers around it, and red-currant jelly separately.

If you have cooked your hare by roasting it (incidentally, remember that it will need plenty of basting if you are cooking it by this method) you may have cold meat to spare. Here is a simple and tasty way of using it.

Grilled Hare

Cut the meat into nice collops, brush with melted butter and season well with salt and cayenne pepper.

Cook under a hot grill, turning frequently, and renewing the melted butter and seasoning from time to time. Serve very hot, with hare gravy and red-currant jelly.

Creamed potatoes or boiled rice can make a border for this dish, if liked.

Here is a recipe written by Anne Hughes, a young farmer's wife, in August 1796. Among a host of other dishes which she prepared for Harvest Home, this one of hares is given in full. It can well be adapted to our more stringent times and makes interesting reading.

Harvest Home Hare

'I didde cooke 3 hares, lyke mye dear mothers waye

After takeinge off their skinnes ande pullinge oute their insides, I didde cutte them upp in peeses, and laye them in milk for one hower, wil I didde choppe uppe 4 apples, 2 unions, and handful off lemmon tyme, sum lemmon rinde, pepper ande salte, and 3 harde boyled eggs, 3 sage leaves ande a tea spoone off browne sugar.

Thys bee all chopped uppe together then I doe putt a laire off peeses off hare in a deepe dish, then cuvver wyth the messe a tabel spoone off watter, then more hare ande sprinkle more off the mixed mess till thee dych bee full.

Pore in 2 wine glasses of porte wine, then when 3 partes full, I doe take 4 egges and bete uppe verie well wyth a tabel spoone off fresh creme, and a littel salt, which I doe pore in thee dyshe after the hare have been cookeing 1 hower ande keepinge itte covvered with a cuvver, ande putting backe until thee eggs bee well sett.

Thys bee verie nice colde.'

Duck Loaf

6 oz minced cooked duck meat	1 tsp. finely grated orange
6 oz minced lean ham	orange peel
4 oz white breadcrumbs	1 tsp. marjoram
2 oz finely chopped mush-room	2 eggs
1 finely chopped onion	Pepper and salt
	Cupful of milk

Blend together all the ingredients, except eggs and milk.
When thoroughly mixed, beat the eggs in the milk, season, and
blend with the rest of the ingredients.

Put into a greased 2 lb loaf tin, pat flat, and bake in a slow to
moderate oven for about an hour. It will begin to come away
from the sides of the tin when done.

Equally good hot or cold.

Try turkey meat done this way, but substitute lemon peel for
orange. A little celery salt helps, too.

Pigeon Pie

The best part of a pigeon, as with all birds, is the breast. Here is
a quick and extravagant way of dealing with 4 pigeons. Take
the kitchen scissors, and cut out the breasts. Pluck them and
clean them and use them in the pie recipe below. Discard the
rest.

If you are horrified by such waste, then pluck and clean the
birds as usual, simmer the remainder of the mutilated corpses
and use for soup, casseroles and other dishes. But, let's face it,
quite often the rest of a pigeon is tough and hardly worth the
trouble of cooking.

8 breasts of pigeon	from the minced liver, onion,
4 fat rashers	mushroom, and breadcrumbs
About ¼ lb forcemeat made	2 hard-boiled eggs

Good short crust pastry using 1 lb flour. You will need
enough to line and cover the pie dish.

Line the pie dish and put a little forcemeat at the bottom.
Chop the fat bacon roughly, and sprinkle a little on top of the
forcemeat. Now place the breasts neatly on top.

Cover breasts with more bacon, slices of hard-boiled egg, and
then another layer of forcemeat. Continue with the layers until
the pie is full, and season well with pepper and salt, between the
layers.

Make sure that the meat is high in the dish. There is an awful lot of earnest advice given about the desirability, or not, of putting in an egg-cup or pie funnel to support a pie lid. If properly packed, the pie really should not need it, but personally I am grateful for any help, and humbly up-end an egg-cup amidst the meat.

Moisten the contents with game stock if you have it, or red wine, which is equally delicious. Put on the lid, and seal the edges well.

Bake in a moderate oven for about an hour.

Carbonnade of Beef

1½ lb lean stewing beef	½ pint brown ale
2 oz beef dripping	½ pint stock
1 large onion	4 rounds of bread
1 clove garlic	Salt, pepper and French mus-
1 oz flour	tard

Cut the beef into neat cubes, and brown quickly in melted dripping. Remove to a casserole.

Fry the sliced onions and crushed garlic till light brown. Put in casserole with the beef.

Drain off surplus fat, and make a good gravy with the flour, stock and ale.

Season to taste and cook gently in a moderate oven for up to 2 hours.

When cooked, spread the rounds of bread with French mustard, and press into the gravy forming a lid. Put back into the oven (without casserole lid) for a further 15 minutes so that the bread can brown a little. This is very sustaining, and particularly welcome in cold weather.

Beef à la Mode

1¼ lb rump steak in the piece
2 rashers of bacon
1½ pints stock
1 onion, carrot, small turnip, parsnip, celery
Bouquet garni

1 oz butter and 1 oz flour for thickening
Glass of red wine, preferably claret
Juice of a lemon
Salt, pepper

Marinade the piece of beef, for at least 2 hours, in a bowl containing the wine, lemon-juice, a little of the onion finely chopped, salt, pepper and bouquet garni.

Melt the butter in a stewpan, dry the beef and fry on each side until brown. Slice the rest of the onion and fry at the same time. Put the meat and onion on one side whilst you make the gravy with the flour, stock and marinade in which the beef was soaked.

Put back the meat and onions and cover with rashers. Slice the vegetables finely and add to the pot.

Simmer for about 2–3 hours. Serve on a hot dish with the sieved vegetables and liquor round it.

Beef Olives

1–1½ lb good stewing beef
(cut in slices less than ½ inch thick)
½ lb forcemeat
1 pint gravy

For the forcemeat, mince 2 or 3 fat rashers and about the same weight of the lean beef. Add a cupful of white breadcrumbs seasoned with salt, pepper and selected herbs, e.g. parsley and thyme. Moisten with a little stock and 1 beaten egg to bind.

Now flatten the beef slices with a few hefty thwacks, and cut into strips about 2 inches by 4 inches. Spread a little forcemeat on each portion and roll up. Tie securely with string and put them in a shallow fireproof dish, covered with the gravy. Simmer for about an hour. Remove the strings when dishing up.

Beef olives can also be made with *cooked* lean beef, in the same way, but the meat must be cut very thin and the dish will need *slower and longer* cooking to be successful.

Jarrett

This can be made with the cheaper cuts of beef such as shin or skirt.

1 lb stewing steak	1 tab. Worcester sauce
¼ lb streaky rashers	1 oz flour
6 sticks of celery	1 oz beef dripping
1 pint brown stock	Black pepper

Cut the steak into small strips. Put each strip on a rasher and roll them up together. Put the rolls into a casserole. Cover with gravy made from stock thickened with beef dripping and flour. Add the Worcester sauce and criss-cross the dish with celery before pouring the gravy into the casserole. Season with black pepper, and just a little salt. The bacon may make this dish salt enough.

Onions, carrots, leeks, etc., can be put in, too. It will take at least 2 hours in a slowish oven.

Steak and Kidney Pudding

In cold weather there are few dishes more welcome than a fine steak and kidney pudding or pie. I particularly like mushrooms added to the meat mixture, but they can be excluded from your pudding and you will still get a delicious dish. If you are feeling really extravagant, oysters can replace the mushrooms. Remember when chopping up the meat, that it is better to chop it rather too finely than to leave the pieces too large, and *keep water boiling*.

For the crust:

> 8 oz plain flour
> 1 heaped tsp. baking powder

3 oz shredded suet
Pinch of salt

For filling:

1 lb stewing steak – rump is best
3 oz ox or lamb kidney
2 oz mushrooms
A little seasoned flour
Stock or water

Grease a 1½-pint-sized pudding basin.

Shred the suet very finely and mix with flour, baking powder and salt. Mix to a rolling consistency with cold water, roll out to a thickness of about ¼ inch. Cut off a third ready for the lid, and line the basin with the rest.

Cut the meat into small pieces and roll in seasoned flour. Arrange in the basin with layers of mushroom, if used, and season with a little salt and black pepper between the layers. A bay leaf, halfway up, improves the flavour.

Add cold water or stock to come within an inch of the top. Moisten the suet crust edges and put on the lid. Seal the edges.

Now cover with greased foil or greased paper, and put into a saucepan of boiling water which reaches halfway up the sides of the pudding basin. Boil for 3½–4 hours and top up the saucepan now and again with *boiling* water.

Bring to the table, in the basin, handsomely swathed in a snowy napkin.

Steak and Kidney Pie

1 lb stewing steak – rump is best
4 oz ox or lamb kidney
Pepper, salt, chopped onion and parsley
Water or stock
6 oz flaky or rough puff or short pastry for lid

Cut the steak into small cubes and the kidney into fine slices. Dust them with seasoned flour, and spread a layer at the bottom of the pie-dish. Sprinkle a little finely chopped onion, parsley, salt and pepper on this layer, and repeat until the pie-dish is full. See that the central part of the meat is well above the level of the dish so that the crust is supported. If in doubt, do as I do and put in a pie funnel to boost the lid and your own morale.

Pour over water or stock to come halfway or three-quarters of the way up the meat.

Roll out the pastry and cover the dish. Make a little hole in the centre for the steam to escape.

Decorate with pastry leaves and gild with brushed beaten egg-yolk. It should be put in a hot oven for about 20 minutes, then lower heat for a further 1½–2 hours. Cover the crust with a piece of foil or paper when you reduce heat, or the crust will get too brown.

If you think that your meat may be a little tough, partly cook it before starting your pie, but remember that it must be cold before putting on the crust.

Do you remember Bo-bo in Charles Lamb's famous 'Dissertation upon Roast Pig'? It was he who was careless enough to burn down his father's house and, worse still, to cause the death by roasting of nine newly farrowed piglets. At that time in China meat was always eaten raw. It was Bo-bo who burnt his fingers on the scorched skin of one of the innocent victims 'and applied them in his booby fashion to his mouth – and for the first time in his life (in the world's life indeed, for before him no man had known it) he tasted – *crackling*!'

Most of us share Bo-bo's enjoyment of crackling. It is perhaps the chief attraction of roast pork. To get crackling really crisp the joint must be put into a hot oven to sear it, a method advocated at one time for all joints of meat when roasting, but now somewhat modified. I am not going to give a recipe for roast pork because it is well-known, but do remember that all pork dishes need thorough cooking and if you *are* roasting pork it will need 35 minutes to each 1 lb of weight plus 35 minutes, longer, in fact, than any other meat, and in a fairly hot oven.

Here are a few warming dishes of pork for cold weather.

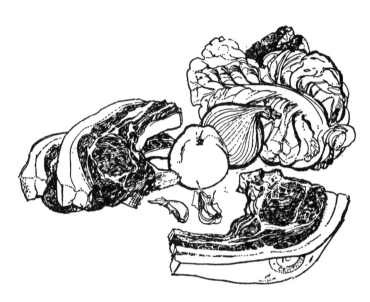

Pork with Red Cabbage

'What else,' I heard a woman say despairingly to the green-grocer, 'can you do with red cabbage besides pickling it?' Here's one answer.

4 good-sized pork chops
¾ pint stock
1 dessertsp. tomato purée
2 tabs. olive oil
1 oz flour
1 onion and clove of garlic

Salt and pepper
1 small red cabbage
1 oz butter
1 apple
1 tab. vinegar
Cup water or stock

Brown the chops in hot oil then place in a casserole. Brown sliced onion and crushed clove of garlic in the oil. Make a roux with the flour, add stock and tomato purée. Stir till the sauce thickens and pour over the chops. Put on the lid and cook for about an hour in a moderate oven.

Shred the cabbage finely. Melt the butter and cook finely sliced apple and onion in it for 5 minutes. When thoroughly coated, add the cabbage, vinegar, stock or water, and season to taste. Simmer, with the lid on, for about an hour. The two dishes take roughly the same time to cook.

Serve the chops on the bed of cooked cabbage. The strained juices can be served separately, or poured over the dish. A garnish of sliced tomatoes or fried onion rings can be added. Hot rice or mashed potato go well with this colourful dish.

Or try a variation of this dish using tomato and green pepper.

Treat the chops as in the first recipe. For the sauce you will need:

> 1 green pepper
> 1 onion
> ¾ lb skinned fresh tomatoes, or
> a tin of Italian variety
> Juice of ½ lemon and a dash of Worcester sauce
> A little stock

Fry sliced onion and pepper (first de-seeded) in the hot fat for about 5 minutes. Add tomatoes, lemon juice, Worcester sauce, stock and seasoning. Cook together for a further 5 minutes, then pour over chops in the casserole. Put on the lid, and cook for an hour in a moderate oven. Serve in the casserole with accompanying vegetables separately.

Here is another way of serving pork chops or cutlets *en casserole*.

Dust both sides of the chops with pepper and salt. Spread the surface with made mustard and leave them in a cool place for an hour or two. Now brown the chops lightly in melted butter or pork fat, put in the casserole, and pour over them a sauce made by thickening the fat, in which they were cooked, with a tablespoonful of flour and a little white wine, such as Graves. A third of a pint should be sufficient.

Put on the lid and cook slowly in a moderate oven for an hour.

Cider and water, in equal quantities, can be used instead of wine.

Italian Pork Cheese

This is a recipe given by the great cook Eliza Acton whose *Modern Cookery for Private Families* was published in 1845, some sixteen years before Mrs Beeton's famous *Book of Household Management* appeared.

She says:

'Chop, not very fine, one pound of lean pork with two pounds of the inside fat; strew over, and mix throughly with them three teaspoonsful of salt, nearly half as much pepper, a half-tablespoonful of mixed parsley, thyme and sage (and sweet-basil, if it can be procured), all minced extremely small. Press the meat closely and evenly into a shallow tin – such as are used for Yorkshire puddings will answer well, – and bake it in a very gentle oven from an hour to an hour and a half: it is served cold in slices.'

She adds:

'Should the proportion of fat be considered too much, it can be diminished on a second trial.'

Most people today, I think, would find it too fatty. I should use equal quantities myself.

It is interesting to note that in her preface to 'Pork Dishes' Eliza Acton stresses the need to check the condition of this meat. She says:

' This meat is so proverbially, and we believe even *dangerously*, unwholesome when ill-fed, or in any degree diseased, that its quality should be closely examined before it is purchased. When not home-reared, it should be bought if possible of some respectable farmer or miller, unless the butcher who supplies it can be perfectly relied on.'

So now you know! I hope that your butcher falls into this category.

Pork Pie

This is a raised pie, which means that you will need Hot Water Pastry made as follows:

Hot Water Pastry:

> 12 oz flour
> Pinch of salt
> 4 oz lard
> Just under a gill of water

Mix the flour and salt together. Put lard and water into a saucepan and bring to the boil. Let it boil for a minute or two. Now pour the mixture into the flour and mix thoroughly until the dough is smooth.

Keep at a gentle heat for about half an hour before using. If it is allowed to get too cool the moulding of the pie will be difficult.

Cut a quarter of the pastry and put on one side, in a warm place, for the lid. Now mould the remaining three-quarters into a pie case. An upturned floured 2-lb jam jar helps here. When the case is high enough and of the right thinness, remove the jar and pack the meat inside, pressing it down firmly as you go.

For the pork pie filling:

> 1 lb lean pork (weighed without bone, gristle, etc.)
> 1 tsp. chopped sage (less if it is dried)
> Pepper and salt
> ¼ oz gelatine
> Beaten egg for gilding

Cut the meat into very small pieces. Mix them with the sage, pepper and salt and pack into the pie. Moisten with about 2 tabs. of pork stock or water.

Keep a small portion of pastry aside for cutting out leaves to decorate the lid. Roll the rest into a circle to fit the top of the pie.

Damp the edges, cover the pie, pinch the edges together, and decorate the top with the pastry leaves. Make sure that there is a hole in the centre before brushing top and sides with the beaten egg. Some people like to snip the edges of the lid with scissors as a further embellishment.

Tie a band of greaseproof paper round the sides of the pie to ensure that it keeps its shape, and bake for 2 hours in a slow to moderate oven. When done, pour in a little stock, in which the gelatine has been dissolved, through the hole in the lid, using a small funnel.

Pork Rissoles

Cooked pork lends itself to mincing very agreeably, possibly because its texture is softer than some other meats. It makes an excellent cottage pie, particularly if a little bacon is added. Try these rissoles, too.

1 lb lean cooked pork	2 oz soft breadcrumbs
1 onion	Dried breadcrumbs and egg
1 egg	for coating
1 tsp. sage	

Mince pork and onion finely, add soft breadcrumbs, sage, seasoning of salt and pepper and blend all together with the beaten egg. A little milk or stock can be added if the mixture is too dry.

Form into balls or round pats. Coat with egg and breadcrumbs and fry until brown in deep fat.

These are excellent with winter green vegetables, or with fresh peas or runner beans in the summer.

Pork Hot-Pot

1 lb fresh belly of pork	2 potatoes
2 onions	1 tsp. chopped sage
2 carrots	1½ pints stock
2 leeks	Flour, pepper and salt

Cut the meat into cubes. Roll them in seasoned flour and fry lightly for a few minutes.

Put a layer of sliced vegetables, including potato, into a casserole. Add the partly cooked pork. Sprinkle with the sage, add the rest of the sliced vegetables, and cover with stock.

Cook in a slow oven for at least 2½ hours.

Little Mutton or Lamb Pies

These used to be great favourites with countrymen returning after a hard day's work in the wintry fields. If the cook was fortunate enough to have any left over, they were just as welcome cold the next day, eaten under a hedge from a red-and-white spotted handkerchief, or from the picnic hamper of the more well-to-do.

The meat can be from any part of the lamb. Good trimmings, not too fat, from shoulder, leg or neck, should be easy to get from the butcher if you tell him your intentions.

1 lb mutton or lamb pieces	For crust:
½ lb potatoes	1 lb plain flour
Pepper and salt	1 tsp. baking powder
Chopped parsley	6 oz beef dripping
1 onion	

Partly boil the potatoes. Chop up the onion and the meat.

Line 8 patty-pans – 10 if small ones – and fill with equal quantities of chopped meat and potato. Sprinkle with onion, salt, pepper and chopped parsley. Cover each with a pastry lid, and cook for ¾–1 hour in a moderate oven. If the tops become brown rather early, spread a piece of foil lightly over the pans. The meat needs quite a little time to cook satisfactorily.

Irish Stew

Too often this is made with meat which is not quite good enough. Neck of lamb is the correct meat, but it is worth buying best end, and for pity's sake be ruthless about cutting off surplus fat. Let the hungry birds have it.

2½ lb best end of neck	2 carrots
2 lb potatoes	Chopped parsley
3 large onions	Pepper and salt

Peel the potatoes and slice them thinly. Put a layer at the bottom of a deep stew-pan. Now put a layer of trimmed neck,

cut into chops, upon the potatoes, then a layer of chopped onions and carrots. Continue with these layers until all is used up. Season with pepper and salt.

Pour in enough stock or water to come about a third or halfway up the saucepan. Bring to the boil, and then simmer gently for about 2 hours. The stew should be quite thick.

Pile it on a hot dish and sprinkle generously with chopped parsley.

Haricot Mutton

1½–2 lb middle neck, or shoulder of mutton	8 oz white haricot beans
3 onions	Dripping, stock and 1 oz flour for gravy
Clove of garlic	8 oz peeled tomatoes or a small tin

Soak the beans overnight – 24 hours is not too long.

Put them with plenty of stock or water into a deep casserole, with an onion stuck with 2 or 3 cloves. Let the beans cook gently in a very slow oven for 1½–2 hours. Strain off liquor for gravy.

Now melt some dripping in a frying-pan, flour the meat which is in small pieces, and fry with the onions until brown. Put them, with the tomatoes, into the casserole with the crushed clove of garlic.

Make a good gravy with the melted dripping and juices in the pan, the flour, pepper and salt. Any liquor from the beans can be used here. Pour over the other ingredients, cover the casserole and simmer for a further 1½ hours.

Farmhouse Chicken Pie

1 semi-cooked chicken
¼ lb ham
3 hard-boiled eggs

Chopped onion, thyme or chervil to flavour
¾–1 lb short or flaky pastry

Simmer chicken in a stew-pot with onion, carrot and a bay leaf. When it is half-cooked, after about 40 minutes, lift from the stew-pot, and slice off the meat. Put a layer at the bottom of the pie-dish, then a layer of ham. Sprinkle lightly with the mixture of finely chopped onion and thyme or chervil between the layers. The hard-boiled eggs should be sliced and form the middle layer.

Moisten with some of the stock in which the bird was cooked and put on the lid of pastry. Remember to make a small hole in the top so that the steam can escape. Glaze with beaten egg, and cook in a moderate oven for 1 hour.

You might like to compare the last recipe with this one written about 1600.

'A Goodlie Pye

Take small chickeyens, break their leggs and brest bones. Make of pastrie the best. Then lay the chickeyens side by side on the pastrie after filling their bellies full of bredcrumbs mixed with fresh butter, parsley, thyme, pepper and salt, wrap pastrie over them, wetting and moulding the edges together.

Bake in a Dutch oven before the fire, turning occasionally, till pastrie is golden, then serve in a deep oval dish, and hand round this Egg and Wine Sauce in a sauceboat along it:

Mix six beaten egg yolks with white wine, vinegar, pepper,

salt, ground cinnamon, sugar and rosewater to taste, and cook till sauce thickens.'

Italian Chicken Casserole

1 chicken, jointed
4 shallots
1 clove garlic
Gill chicken stock

¼ lb mushrooms
1 tsp. white sugar
3 tabs: tomato purée
1 glass medium sherry
Pepper and salt

Melt the butter, flour the joints and brown them in the butter. Put them aside.

Now add the roughly chopped shallots, mushrooms and crushed garlic. Simmer gently for about 5 minutes. Now add the tomato purée, sherry, chicken stock and sugar. Finally, put in the chicken joints and simmer until tender. This will take about 30–40 minutes.

Put the joints on a hot serving dish and pour the sauce over them. Sprinkle with chopped parsley, or garnish with lemon wedges or watercress.

This can be served with a border of hot creamed potato or rice, or the vegetables can be served separately.

Chicken Pilaff

1 lb cooked chicken
½ lb long grain rice
1 large onion
1 pint stock
1 tab. olive oil or melted butter

1 tab. chopped parsley
1 tab. chopped basil
¼ lb fresh peas
2 oz cheese
Seasoning

Put rice, onion, herbs and peas to simmer in the stock. They should take about 15 minutes to cook. Remove from heat.

Now stir in chopped chicken, salt and pepper to taste and the oil or butter. Blend well, and put into a fireproof dish. Sprinkle grated cheese on top, and bake for about 15 minutes in a moderate oven.

Chicken Terrine

1 chicken
½ lb belly of pork
1 shallot
1 clove of garlic crushed

½ tsp. celery salt
½ tsp. allspice
6 rashers streaky bacon
Butter for greasing

Cut the breasts of the chicken into thin slices. Mince the rest with the pork, shallot and seasoning.

Butter a terrine, or fireproof straight-sided casserole, and put 3 rashers at the bottom. On top of these put a layer of the minced meat and then a layer of chicken slices and the remaining rashers.

Continue to fill the terrine with alternate layers of the mince and chicken slices, finishing with the mince.

Place in a bain-marie, or roasting tin half full of water, and cook in a slow oven for about 1½–2 hours.

Pour off excess fat, and put a weight on top as it cools. Serve cold in the terrine.

Chicken with Grape Sauce

1 chicken
1 onion
1 carrot
Bouquet garni
½ lb sultana grapes or white grapes

2 oz butter
2 oz flour
Dessertsp. curry powder
4 tabs. double cream
Salt and pepper

Simmer the chicken with the onion, carrot and bouquet garni, for about an hour or until tender. Remove it, strain the stock and allow this to cool so that the fat can easily be lifted off.

Cut the flesh into nice-sized pieces and put in a warm dish.

Wash the grapes. If they are sultana grapes with delicate skins and no pips, you are home and dry. If you are using ordinary white grapes, then you must skin and pip them.

Make the sauce by melting the butter and stirring in the flour and the curry powder, in the usual way, adding gradually a pint of the chicken stock. Stir until it thickens. Now drop in the grapes. Finally, remove from heat, add the cream, pour over the chicken and serve.

Boiled Chicken with Rice

1 chicken – preferably not a a broiler bird	1 lemon
1 onion	8 oz rice
1 carrot	Bouquet garni
2 sticks celery	Stock or water to cover bird
	Salt and pepper

Put a slice or two of onion inside the bird before trussing. Put it into a large saucepan covered with white stock or water, add sliced vegetables and bouquet garni and simmer until tender – about 2 hours.

Lift out the bird and keep hot while the rice is being cooked. Tip the rice into about three-quarters of a pint of the simmering chicken liquor and cook for 12–14 minutes. Strain, if need be, put on the serving dish and arrange the chicken, nicely carved into portions, upon it. Serve with white sauce made with equal parts of milk and chicken liquor.

Russian Cabbage

We are not very adventurous with cabbages, but here is a recipe which is simple, tasty, and useful for using up cooked meat, and gives cabbage a new look.

A firm cabbage	White stock
Minced cooked meat chicken is very good	Glass of white wine
1 lemon	Salt and pepper

Cut the cabbage in half and cut out the tough stalk. Use only the fairly large inner leaves. Place them separately in a large bowl and pour over them some boiling water. Leave for a few minutes to soften.

Season the minced meat and moisten slightly with stock or wine. Fill each half leaf with this, roll it up and skewer with a cherry stick.

Place the roll in a shallow fireproof dish. Squeeze lemon juice over them, then add glassful of white wine, and use stock to cover the cabbage rolls.

Cook, with the lid on, in a moderate oven until tender – about 30–40 minutes.

The classic tripe and onions can be found in any cookery book, but here are one or two other methods of cooking this nourishing offal.

Tripe Mornay

1½ lb tripe	1 oz flour
½ pint milk	4 oz grated cheese
1 oz butter	Salt and pepper
	Juice of 1 lemon

Cut tripe into strips or squares. Blanch by putting into cold water and bringing to the boil and simmering for a couple of minutes.

Drain off this water, and add enough fresh to cover the tripe. Squeeze in the juice of the lemon. Simmer gently for an hour.

Make a cheese sauce with melted butter, thickened with flour, the milk and seasoning. Add the grated cheese to this, stirring well. Lift the tripe from the water, place it in a hot dish and pour the cheese sauce over it.

Sprinkle with chopped chives, parsley or paprika.

Tripe à la Lyonnaise

1½ lb cold cooked tripe	Dessertsp. wine vinegar
2 oz butter	Dessertsp. chopped parsley
1 large onion	Salt and pepper

Heat the butter in a frying pan. Slice the onion and fry until soft and turning golden.

Cut the tripe into small neat squares and add to the pan. Then put in the vinegar, seasoning and parsley. Turn the contents of the pan several times so that all are thoroughly heated. This will take 10–15 minutes. Serve very hot, with hot rice, mashed potato and selected vegetables.

Tripe à la Portugaise

1½ lb tripe	2 oz flour
3 large onions	1 tsp. oregano
4 tabs. concentrated tomato purée	Clove of garlic
	1 pint stock or water
2 oz butter	Salt and cayenne pepper

Cut the blanched tripe into slices, and dredge well with flour seasoned with oregano.

Melt the butter in the casserole in which the dish will be served. Put in the floured tripe, and let it cook gently for about 10 minutes. Add the sliced onions and the crushed clove of garlic.

Thicken with the flour and tomato purée, smoothing out any lumps, and add gently the stock or water. Season with salt and cayenne to taste.

Cover and cook in a slow oven for 2½–3 hours.

Sweets

Lemon Mousse

This is a most refreshing sweet, and a general favourite. If however you find lemons a little too sharp, then make an *orange mousse* in exactly the same way, substituting 3 oranges for the 3 lemons in the recipe.

> 3 lemons
> 3 eggs
> 4 oz caster sugar
> ½ oz gelatine

Dissolve gelatine in half a cupful of warm water. Grate the rind from 2 of the lemons.

Separate the whites from the yolks of the eggs and beat the yolks with the sugar until creamy. An electric beater helps here. Add the grated rind and the juice of all 3 lemons gradually.

Now stir in the gelatine and strain all into a clean bowl. Beat the egg whites until stiff, and fold into the mixture.

Transfer to a soufflé dish and chill well before serving.

Dundee Tart

This is really a less cloying version of treacle tart, using half marmalade and half golden syrup for the filling. Marmalade alone makes a very nice filling for an open tart.

For 4 people you will need:

> 6 oz plain flour
> 3 oz butter
> ½ tsp. sugar

For filling:

 2 large tabs. golden syrup
 2 large tabs. marmalade
 1 tsp. lemon juice
 1 beaten egg

Make the short crust, line tin or pie plate and bake blind for 10 minutes in a hot oven. Remove paper and contents, and cool pastry case slightly.

Warm marmalade and syrup, and mix together with beaten egg and lemon juice. Put into the case and cook in a moderate oven for about 20–25 minutes.

N.B. To 'bake blind' put a piece of greased paper, greasy side down, into the tin and fill it with haricot beans, macaroni pieces or something similar. Then bake for 10–15 minutes. When done remove paper and filling.

Ginger Pudding

On a cold day this is a very welcome pudding.

 For 4 generous helpings:

½ lb plain flour
1 tsp. ground ginger
1 level tsp. bicarbonate of soda
1 tab. treacle

1 egg
4 oz finely shredded suet
3 oz caster sugar
Milk

Sift flour, ginger and soda into a bowl, and add the sugar and shredded suet. Stir in the beaten egg and treacle, adding enough milk to make a soft mixture which will drop from a spoon.

Put into a well-greased 2-pint basin. Cover with foil or grease-proof paper and steam for 2 hours.

The addition of a little chopped stem ginger adds a nice piquancy to this pudding.

Hot apple sauce is good with this, or Syrup Sauce.

Syrup Sauce

> 4 oz brown sugar
> ½ pint water
> 1 tsp. lemon juice
> 1 tsp. arrowroot

Dissolve sugar in the water. Blend arrowroot and lemon juice with a spoonful of cold water and thicken the sauce with it.

Some chopped preserved ginger can be simmered in the sauce for extra flavouring, and the syrup from a jar of preserved ginger can be substituted for a proportion of the water used.

Crème Brûlée

I first came across this exquisite sweet at the Dorothy Restaurant in Cambridge. I was eighteen at the time, and decided then and there that no other sweet could touch it. So far, I have not changed my opinion.

For 4 generous helpings:

> 1 pint single cream
> 6 egg yolks
> 1–2 tabs. caster sugar – vanilla-flavoured if possible
> 2–3 tabs. granulated or caster sugar for caramel top

Put the cream into a double saucepan and bring to the boil. Meanwhile beat caster sugar and egg yolks together. Pour the hot cream into this mixture, return all to the double boiler and stir until it thickens.

Put it into a greased fireproof dish and cook in a very slow oven for about 20–30 minutes.

The cream should now be thoroughly set. Remove from oven and allow it to get cold.

Sprinkle granulated or caster sugar thickly and smoothly over the surface. Put it under a very hot grill until the sugar turns brown and melts.

Remove from heat and allow it to cool. This dish is best when chilled for an hour or so before serving.

Zabaglione

To make 4 helpings you will need:

    3 egg yolks
    3 tabs. caster sugar
    3 tabs. Madeira, Marsala or sweet sherry

Lodge a basin over a saucepan of hot water. Put in egg yolks and sugar and whisk until the mixture is creamy in colour and consistency.

Add the wine gradually and stir slowly. The mixture should be firm enough to take the impression of the back of a spoon. Be careful not to over cook it or it may curdle.

Spoon the mixture into individual glasses and serve at once with Boudoir biscuits or wafer biscuits.

Winter Rice Pudding

This is a useful and slightly more interesting version of the good plain rice pudding. It cooks well in a very slow oven and is ideal when you are cooking a casserole dish for the main course.

2 oz rice
2 oz sugar
1 oz butter
1 pint milk

Rind of 1 lemon
1 oz seedless raisins or sultanas
1 oz candied peel
1 oz chopped glacé cherries

Put milk, rice, sugar and butter into a greased pie dish.
Stir in the dried fruit and finely grated lemon rind.

Cook very slowly in a gentle oven for 2 hours at least. Stir once or twice during cooking to improve texture.

When fresh fruit is hard to come by, this pudding is a useful stand-by.

Syllabub (1)

½ pint double cream
2 tabs. caster sugar
1 lemon
¼ pint white wine
2 tabs. brandy

Grate the lemon. Put the grated rind, lemon juice, sugar and brandy into the white wine. Cover, and put into cool place overnight.

In the morning, make sure that the sugar has dissolved, then strain the liquid.

To this add the cream, and whisk *gently by hand,* until it is thick. Time for this varies considerably, so go gently.

Put into small individual glasses and serve with *tuiles* or Boudoir biscuits.

Remember that this is exceptionally rich. It is better to look mingy and give one's guests too little rather than too much at the end of a meal. These amounts will serve 6 people easily.

Syllabub (2)

½ pint double cream
2 tabs. caster sugar
1 lemon
6 macaroons

Small wineglass of Maderia, Marsala or fruit sherry
Pinch ground cinnamon or nutmeg

Put the macaroons at the base of the dish in which you will serve the syllabub.

Mix together the grated rind and juice of the lemon, sugar, wine, cinnamon or nutmeg. If you can let it stand for an hour, all the better. Now add the cream.

Whip all *by hand* to the frothy stage, and add little by little by the spoonful to the macaroons in the bowl, until the bowl is full. Chill well before serving.

Cakes

Gingerbread Sponge

This is one of my favourite winter recipes. The sponge keeps well and is a beautiful dark colour.

You will need:

10 oz flour
½ oz ground ginger
1 tsp. mixed spice
½ lb golden syrup

3 oz brown sugar
4 oz butter or lard
2 eggs
2 tabs. milk
1 tsp. bicarbonate of soda

Put butter, milk and syrup into a large saucepan to melt together slowly.

Put all the dry ingredients into a bowl. Dissolve the bicarbonate of soda in a little milk, and beat the eggs.

Now tip the dry ingredients into the melted contents of the saucepan. Mix well. Add the drop of milk, in which the soda is dissolved, and the beaten eggs. Beat all together thoroughly.

Pour into a shallow greased and floured baking tin, or into two sandwich tins and bake for 45 minutes in a moderate oven.

If you have any preserved ginger, add some, finely chopped, to the mixture. Some people add a few seedless raisins.

Cinnamon can be substituted for the ground ginger and makes a pleasant change.

Grasmere Gingerbread

1 lb flour
1 tsp. each cream of tartar and bicarbonate of soda
½ lb Barbadoes sugar (the very dark soft kind)
½ lb butter
1 tab. golden syrup (2 if a hard gingerbread is liked)
Dessertsp. ground ginger
Pinch of salt

Cream together butter and sugar, add syrup and dry ingredients. It will be dry and crumbly, but don't add any liquid.

Put the gingerbread into a well-greased tin to a depth of 1½ inches. Press lightly with the back of a spoon.

Cook in a very slow oven for at least 1 hour. It should not need more than 1½ hours.

The gingerbread will be crumbly on top but firm below. Remember to cut it into pieces before it gets cold.

Ginger Nuts

8 oz plain flour
Dessertsp. ground ginger
8 oz Demerara or Barbadoes sugar
4 oz butter

2 eggs
Small tsp. bicarbonate of soda
2 tabs. milk

Dissolve soda in the milk and add the 2 well-beaten eggs.

In another basin mix all dry ingredients together, and then rub in the butter. Add milk, soda and eggs and blend well.

The mixture should be soft.

Now flour your hands and form the mixture into walnut-sized balls, and place them well apart on a greased baking sheet. Flatten the tops a little. They should spread into a neat circle as they cook.

Store in an air-tight tin when cold. Some people put a split almond on top of each before the biscuits are baked, and very nice too.

Cheese Scones

Try these at tea-time on a raw winter's day.

> 6 oz self-raising flour
> 2 oz butter
> 2 oz grated cheddar cheese
> Pinch of salt
> Sour or fresh milk to mix

Rub the butter into the flour and salt until the mixture is like breadcrumbs.

Add grated cheese, and mix to a dough with the milk. Roll out to a depth of about ½ inch, cut into small circles and bake in a hot oven for 10–15 minutes.

Split and butter when cool enough, and eat whilst still warm.

Preserves

Orange Marmalade

One of the most cheering things about the cheerless month of January is the making of marmalade. The fragrance of simmering golden fruit from sunny lands is almost as rewarding as the filled pots themselves.

I find that it is quicker and far less messy to cook the oranges first. This recipe is reliable and yields about 7 lb which suits my sized household perfectly.

> 12 Seville oranges
> 3 pints water

5 lb preserving sugar
2 lemons

Wash oranges and simmer in 2 pints of the water until soft. Remove oranges when cool and cut in half. Keep the water in which they are cooked.

Take out pith and pips, and simmer in the remaining pint of water in another saucepan, for 15–20 minutes.

Now chop the cooked peel finely or thickly according to taste. Return to pan with the water in which the oranges were cooked. Add sugar, juice and grated rind of the lemons and the strained liquid from pith and pips.

Allow sugar to dissolve over gentle heat, stirring the while. Then boil rapidly until a set is obtained, which should take about 25 minutes, skimming as the scum rises.

Let the marmalade cool slightly before pouring into warm jars.

Two tablespoons of an orange liqueur such as Cointreau or Aurum can be added at this stage. The same amount of whisky can be used instead, and adds a heartening fillip to a winter's breakfast.

One year I missed the Seville oranges and substituted Italian bitter oranges instead in this recipe. If anything, I liked the flavour better.

To my mind, cooking is the most creative and rewarding part of house-keeping. Always bear in mind the golden truth that a dish should *taste of itself*, that is, of its main ingredients.

Take time in choosing those ingredients, and in preparing them. If you set out to enjoy the different stages of your art, then you will surely get . . . and give . . . a great deal of happiness.

INDEX